BEFORE FREEDOM,
WHEN I JUST CAN REMEMBER

Other books by Belinda Hurmence

Tough Tiffany
A Girl Called Boy
Tancy
My Folks Don't Want Me to Talk about Slavery
The Nightwalker

BEFORE FREEDOM,
WHEN I JUST CAN REMEMBER

Twenty-seven Oral Histories of Former South Carolina Slaves

Edited by Belinda Hurmence

John F. Blair, Publisher
Winston-Salem, North Carolina

Cover photograph—

Brutus, an ex-slave at his home on Palawana Island.

From the Penn School Collection.
Courtesy of Penn Center, Inc.,
St. Helena Island, South Carolina.

Library of Congress Cataloging-in-Publication Data

Before freedom, when I just can remember : twenty-seven oral histories
   of former South Carolina slaves / edited by Belinda Hurmence.
      p.   cm.
   Bibliography: p.
   ISBN 0-89587-069-X : $8.95 (est.)
   1. Slaves—South Carolina—Biography. 2. Afro-Americans—South
Carolina—Biography. 3. South Carolina—Biography. 4. Slavery—
South Carolina—History—Sources. 5. Oral history.   I. Hurmence,
Belinda.
E445.S7B44   1989
975.6′00496073022—dc19   89-243
[B]   CIP

for Joanne Bailey Wilson

Contents

INTRODUCTION

America's infamous period of slavery casts a long shadow on our national past, a shadow in which those human beings who were most affected are still but dimly perceived. History may readily assess the economics and politics that condemned an entire race to bondage for nearly 250 years, but it continues to conceal from us the *slave* trapped in slavery. After all, history as we know it, is the written record of a people, and the black slaves of America were, by law, illiterate. The writings of Frederick Douglass, Booker T. Washington, and a few others are scarcely representative of the four million slaves who attained Freedom only after a bitter and bloody civil war.

How, then, 125 years after the fact, can Americans learn about the lives of those four million before and after Freedom?

During the Great Depression of the 1930s, various government agencies initiated work programs across the country to provide jobs for the unemployed. The Library of Congress supervised the program conceived for jobless writers. One of the projects it undertook culminated in *Slave Narratives*, a collection of black folk histories.

The Federal Writers' Project sent field workers to interview blacks who had lived under slavery and recalled their experiences of it. Most of the ex-slaves were found in the South, although a sizeable number reported from states not generally regarded as southern. The project yielded oral histories on a scale unprecedented at the time.

In a time before the tape recorder, the field workers asked the former slaves a list of questions devised for the project and wrote out the answers. The interviews were compiled. Ten thousand pages of typed manuscript, representing some two thousand voices, were placed in storage in the Library of Congress.

Vivid voices they were, too, at last having their say about that murky time "before Freedom."

Sylvia Cannon, former slave of "Old Marster Bill Briggs," in Florence County: "At night the overseer would walk out to see could he catch any of us walking without a note, and to this day, I don't want to go nowhere without a paper."

Fannie Griffin, ex-slave of Joe Beard in Columbia, South Carolina: "I think about my old mammy heap of times now and how I's seen her whipped, with the blood dripping off of her."

The concept of bondage has always fascinated free Americans. With slavery more than a century behind us, and beyond the recollection of any living person, the fascination still persists. Perhaps the invisible, traumatic ties that bind us evoke a dread empathy with the physically enslaved. Scholars, researchers, and writers have always felt the tug of emotions adherent to the *Slave Narratives*.

They have also felt bewildered by the material. For one thing, there is so much of it. For another, it is so uneven, sometimes joyous, sometimes bitter in tone. Some of the ex-slaves were more articulate than others. The expertise of the field workers in committing personalities to paper varied greatly.

The collection remained virtually untouched for years. In time, the Library of Congress microfilmed the entire ten thousand pages to make it more accessible to scholars. In more time, facsimile pages came to be published in multi-volume editions.

Twelve years ago, in gathering background material for a novel I was then writing, I discovered the *Slave Narratives*. Although I found the testimonies uneven, and the very bulk of them daunting, I saw at once the treasure that lay in the oral histories. The *Narratives* resounded with an authenticity I had not encountered before in any prose dealing with slavery. I set aside my novel and read on. It took me two years to read through the collection, and I ended up with a file of notes thick enough to fill a dozen novels. I subsequently wrote two, based on my notes.

The emotional content of the *Narratives* convinced me that they should be accessible to casual readers as well as to scholars and historians. Thus, I came to edit a selection, first from the North Carolina *Narratives*, and now, as a companion volume, from the South Carolina voices.

The bucolic image of slaves living in contentment on the southern plantation has for years been labeled stereotypical. In the South Carolina *Narratives*, we may find over and over what appears to be a reinforcement of the label. Nostalgia veils many memories for the former slaves.

"Times was sure better long time ago than they be now," says Sylvia Cannon.

While Peter Clifton from Kershaw County and the plantation of Biggers Mobley reports, "Yes, sir, us had a bold, driving, pushing marster, but not a hard-hearted one."

Of course, more than nostalgia cloaks South Carolina's ex-slaves. Age, for one thing was a factor; all the speakers were old. Old and poor. They made it into the 1930s, but a lot of them suffered the declining health that stalks old age and poverty. They also suffered the hopelessness of the Great Depression then blanketing their world. Through the scrim of the seventy intervening years, it was easy for them to view their past lives in bondage as a time of plenty, a time when pleasures were simple and their youthful energies high, a time when plantation life meant shelter, food, medical care.

Why is there no pervasive cry of rage from the former bondsmen? Why instead these protestations of affection for a condition which shames the civilized world?

It is useful to remember that Freedom, following the Civil War, brought virtually no improvement in the lives of the liberated. The former slaves knew themselves to be free, but they also recognized their powerlessness. Reconstruction had shattered their embryonic political aspirations. They had felt safer— they had undoubtedly *lived* safer—in the fiefdom of their former masters. Uneducated and ignorant of the world outside the plantation, oppressed by the law, intimidated by night riders and Klansmen, few could see Freedom as a condition to be cherished.

And little support came from their former defenders, the victors in the recent hostilities. The war-weary Yankees had lost interest in the high principle for which they had fought. Like their southern counterparts, they focused their efforts on rebuilding the strained economy, and left the new citizens to endure Freedom much as they had endured slavery.

Thus, field hands who had been exploited as slaves were abandoned to exploitation as sharecroppers. Merely to subsist, women who had been house slaves continued cooking and cleaning during the day and took in washing at night. A century would pass before the civil rights advances of the 1960s appreciably altered their lot.

The reader of these oral histories also should bear in mind that the former slaves responded to a white questioner, and as in bygone days, by lifelong habit said what they believed the one in authority wished to hear. They used "jaw sense," as the adage held in time of slavery. The more outspoken individuals would probably have fled the plantation before these interviews were collected, just as those early militants, the runaway slaves, did before Freedom. Thus we must view the *Narratives* as somewhat weighted, however subtly.

The field workers who recorded *Slave Narratives* for the Federal Writers' Project had instructions to register the individual's dialect in transcribing their interviews. From the practice, a colorful, free-wheeling speech emerges to delight us, as the language of an oral culture nearly always does.

"My eyes does be pretty good, 'cause dey got on dey second glove," declares one aged South Carolinian.

But verbatim dialect also renders, unfortunately, a tedious prose. Apostrophes spatter the page; tortuous spellings abound. To enhance readability, I have eliminated from the present selection many of the elisions and misspellings of the original, relying on local idiom to convey the subjects' style of speech. Even so, the Gullah talk of South Carolina's sea islands often eluded me, and I had to scratch for narratives of the coastal region that would still make sense to the reader. The ex-slave Ben Horry's phrase, "before Freedom, when I just can remember," from its very clarity, beams like a beacon through the thick dialect of Murrell's Inlet.

I have not corrected the grammar of my selections, but I have made cuts of repetitious or extraneous material. I have also rearranged the order of some passages, particularly in the longer narratives. My aim in so doing has been to impose a chronology upon the account, never to alter the speaker's meaning. Bracketed material within the text represents editorial comment or explanation.

In South Carolina, 284 ex-slaves told their stories for the Federal Writers' Project, their contributions totaling more than twelve hundred typewritten pages of manuscript. My choice of twenty-seven narratives for this volume involved a number of considerations, content being paramount. I looked for a diverse range of locations, the better to show the prevailing treatment of slaves wherever they lived. I selected by gender, to accommodate the viewpoints of both women and men, and by age.

The narrators quoted here were at least ten years old at the time they were freed. They had all reached their

80s and 90s when interviewed in the 1930s. To rely on the recollections of children who had been much younger than ten, I judged, risked hearsay, and I wished to present only firsthand statements.

I have indicated the interview age of the ex-slave at the beginning of each narrative in this book, and the address, when that was available. Little can be inferred from this meager supplement, beyond the fact that, in the 1930s, seventy years after their liberation, South Carolina's ex-slaves were still living on or near the plantation, and much the same as they always had lived, before Freedom.

Belinda Hurmence

BEFORE FREEDOM,
WHEN I JUST CAN REMEMBER

VIOLET GUNTHARPE

Age 82, when interviewed by
W. W. Dixon, in Winnsboro, S.C.

I was born a slave in the Rocky Mount part of Fair-field County, up close to Great Falls. I hear them falls a-roaring now, and I see them waters flashing in the sunshine when I close my eyes.

My pappy name Robert and my mammy name Phyllis. They belong to the old-time aristocrats, the Gaither family. Does you know Miss Mattie Martin, which was the secretary of Governor Ansel? That one of my young missuses [also referred to as "mistress" and "old miss" in the *Slave Narratives*] and another is that pretty red-headed girl in the telegraph office at Winnsboro, that just sit there and pass out lightning and electricity over the wires wheresomever she take a notion. Before their mama marry Marster Starke Martin, her was Sally Gaither, my young missus in slavery time. Her die and go to Heaven last year, please God.

Marster Richard was a good marster [master; also referred to as "massa," "Maussa," "mass," and "marse"] to his slaves, though he took no foolishness and worked you from sun to sun. 'Spect him had about ten family of slaves and about fifty big and little slaves altogether on that plantation before them Yankees come and make a mess out of their lives.

Honey, us wasn't ready for the big change that come. Us had no education, no land, no mule, no cow, not a pig, nor a chicken, to set up housekeeping. The birds had nests in the air, the foxes had holes in the ground, and the fishes had beds under the great falls, but us colored folks was left without any place to lay our heads.

The Yankees sure throwed us in the briar patch, but us not bred and born there like the rabbit. Us born in a good log house. The cows was down there in the canebrakes to give us milk; the hogs was fattening on hickory nuts, acorns, and shucked corn to give us meat and grease; the sheep with their wool and the cotton in the gin house was there to give us clothes. The horses and mules was there to help that corn and cotton, but when them Yankees come and take all that away, all us had to thank them for, was a hungry belly, and Freedom. Something us had no more use for then, than I have today for one of them airplanes I hears flying round the sky, right now.

Well, after ravaging the whole countryside, the army got across old Catawba and left the air full of the stink of dead carcasses and the sky black with turkey buzzards. The white women was weeping in hushed voices, the niggers on the place not knowing what to do next, and the pickaninnies sucking their thumbs for want of something to eat. Mind you 'twas wintertime too.

Lots of the chillun die, as did the old folks, while the rest of us scour the woods for hickory nuts, acorns, cane roots, and artichokes, and seine the river for fish. The worst nigger men and women follow the army. The balance settle down with the white folks and simmer in their misery all through the springtime, till plums, mulberries, and blackberries come, and the shad come up the Catawba River.

My mammy stay on with the same marster till I was grown, that is fifteen, and Thad got to looking at me, meek as a sheep and dumb as a calf. I had to ask that nigger right out what his intentions was, before I get him to bleat out that he love me. Him name Thad Guntharpe.

I glance at him one day at the pigpen when I was slopping the hogs. I say, "Mr. Guntharpe, you follows me night and morning to this pigpen; do you happen to be in love with one of these pigs? If so, I'd like to know which one 'tis. Then sometime I come down here by myself and tell that pig about your affections."

Thad didn't say nothing but just grin. Him took the slop bucket out of my hand and look at it, all round it, put upside down on the ground, and set me down on it. Then, he fall down there on the grass by me and blubber out and warm my fingers in his hands.

I just took pity on him and told him mighty plain that he must limber up his tongue and ask something, say what he mean, wanting to visit them pigs so often.

Us carry on foolishness about the little boar shoat pig and the little sow pig, then I squeal in laughter. The slop bucket tipple over and I lost my seat. That ever remain the happiest minute of my eighty-two years.

After us marry, us moved on the Johnson place and Thad plow right on a farm where there use to be a town of Grimkeville. I was lonely down there all the time. I's halfway scared to death of the skeeters about my legs in daytime and old Captain Thorn's ghost in the nighttime.

You never heard about that ghost? If you went to school to Mr. Luke Ford sure he must of tell you about the time a slave boy killed his marster, Old Captain Thorn. He drag and throwed his body in the river.

When they find his body, they catch John, the slave boy, give him a trial by six white men, find him guilty, and he confess. Then, they took the broad axe, cut off his head, mount it on a pole, and stick it up on the bank where they find Old Captain Thorn.

That pole and head stay there till it rot down. Captain Thorn's ghost appear and disappear along that river bank ever since. My pappy tell me he see it and see the boy's ghost, too.

The ghost rode the minds of many colored folks. Some say that the ghost had a heap to do with deaths on that river, by drowning. One sad thing happen: the ghost and the malaria run us off the river.

Us moved to Marster Starke P. Martin's place. Him was a-setting at a window in the house one night, and somebody crept up there and fill his head full of buckshot. Marster Starke was Miss Sallie's husband, and Miss Mattie and Miss May's papa. Oh, the misery of that night to my white folks! Who did it? God knows! They sent poor Henry Nettles to the penitentiary for it, but most white folks and all the colored didn't believe he done it. White folks say a white man done it, but our color knew it was the work of that slave boy's ghost.

Did you ever read about foots of ghosts? They got foots and can jump and walk. No, they don't run. Why? 'Cause seem like their foots is too big. That night Marster Starke Martin was killed it was a-snowing. The whole earth was covered with a white blanket. It snowed and snowed and snowed. Us measure how big that snow was next morning and how big that ghost track.

The snow was seven inches and a little bit deep. The ghost track on top the snow big as a elephant's. Him or she or its tracks appear to drop with the snow and just rise up out the snow and disappear. The white folks say 'twas a man with bags on his foots, but they never found the bags, so I just believe it was ghost instigated by the devil to drop down there and make all that misery for my white folks.

My white folks come here from Maryland, I heard them say. They fought in the Revolution, set up a tanyard when they got here, and then when cotton come, my marster's pappy was the first to put up a horse-gin and screw pit in Rocky Mount section. I glories in their blood, but there's none by the name around here now, 'cept colored folks.

There's a great day a-coming, when the last trumpet will sound and the devil and all the ghosts will be chained and they can't romp around the old river and folks' houses in the nighttime and bring sorrow and pain in the wake of them big tracks.

BRAWLEY GILMORE

*Interviewed by Caldwell Sims at
34 Hamlet Street, Union, S.C.;
December 1936.*

We lived in a log house during the Ku Klux days. They would watch you just like a chicken rooster watching for a worm. At night, we was scared to have a light. They would come around with the "dough faces" on, and peer in the windows, and open the door. If you didn't look out, they would scare you half to death.

John Good, a darky blacksmith, used to shoe the horses for the Ku Klux. He would mark the horseshoes with a bent nail or something like that; then after a raid, he could go out in the road and see if a certain horse had been rode. So, he began to tell on the Ku Klux.

As soon as the Ku Klux found out they was being give away, they suspicioned John. They went to him and made him tell how he knew who they was. They kept him in hiding; and when he told his tricks, they killed him.

When I was a boy on the Gilmore place, the Ku Klux would come along at night a-riding the niggers like they was goats. Yes, sir, they had them down on all-fours a-crawling, and they would be on their backs.

They would carry the niggers to Turk Creek bridge and make them set up on the bannisters of the bridge. Then, they would shoot them offen the bannisters into the water. I declare them was the awfulest days I ever is seed.

A darky name Sam Scaife drifted a hundred yards in the water downstream. His folks took and got him outen that bloody water and buried him on the bank of the creek. The Ku Klux would not let them take him to no graveyard. Fact is, they would not let many of the niggers take the dead bodies of the folks nowhere. They just throwed them in a big hole right there and pulled some dirt over them. For weeks after that, you could not go near that place, because it stink so far and bad.

Sam's folks, they throwed a lot of "Indian-head" rocks all over his grave, 'cause it was so shallow, and them rocks kept the wild animals from a-bothering Sam. You can still see them rocks. I could carry you there right now.

Another darky, Eli McCollum, floated about three-and-a-half miles down the creek. His folks went there and took him out and buried him on the banks of the stream right by the side of a Indian mound. You can see that Indian mound to this very day. It is big as my house is, over there on the Chester side.

The Ku Klux and the niggers fit at New Hope Church. A big rock marks the spot today. The church, it done burnt down. The big rock sets about seven miles east of

Lockhart on the road to Chester. The darkies killed some of the Ku Klux and they took their dead and put them in Pilgrims' Church. Then, they set fire to that church and it burnt everything up to the very bones of the white folks. And ever since then, that spot has been known as Burnt Pilgrim. The darkies left most of the folks right there for the buzzards and other wild things to eat up. Because them niggers had to get away from there; and they didn't have no time for to fetch no word or nothing to no folks at home.

They had a hiding place not far from Burnt Pilgrim. A darky name Austin Sanders, he was carrying some victuals to his son. The Ku Klux catch him and they asked him where he was a-going. He allowed that he was a-setting some bait for coons. The Ku Klux took and shot him and left him lying right in the middle of the road with a biscuit in his dead mouth.

Dr. McCollum was one of them Ku Klux, and the Yankees set out for to catch him. Doc, he rid a white pony called Fannie. Doc, he liked to fiddle. Old Fannie, she would get up on her hind legs when the doc would play his fiddle. All the darkies, they love Doc, so they would help him for to get away from the Yankees, even though he was a Ku Klux.

It's one road what forks, after you cross Woods Ferry. Don't nobody go over that old road now. One fork go to Leeds and one to Chester. Well, right in this fork, Mr. Buck Worthy had done built him a grave in the Woods Ferry Graveyard.

It was built out of marble and it was covered up with a marble slab. Mr. Worthy, he would take and go there and open it up and get in it on pretty days.

So old Doc, he knowed about that grave. He was going to see a sick lady one night when some Yankees got after him. He was on old Fannie. They was about to catch the old Doc when he reached in sight of that graveyard. It was dark. So Doc, he drive the horse on past the fork, and then he stop and hitch her in front of some dense pines.

Then, he went to that grave, slip that top slab back, got in there, and pulled it over him, just leaving a little crack. Doc allowed he wrapped up hisself in his horse blanket, and when the Yankees left, he went to sleep in that grave and never even woke up till the sun, it was a-shining in his face.

Soon after that, my sister took down sick with the misery. Doc, he come to see her at night. He would hide in the woods in daytime. We would fetch him his victuals. My sister was sick three weeks before she died. Doc, he would take some blankets and go and sleep in that grave, 'cause he knowed they would look in our house for him. They kept on a-coming to our house. Course, we never knowed nothing about no doctor at all.

There was a nigger with wooden bottom shoes, that stuck to them Yankees and other poor white trash around there. He allowed with his big mouth that he going to find the doctor. He told it that he had seed Fannie in the graveyard at night.

Us heard it and told the doctor. Us did not want him to go near that graveyard anymore. But Doc, he just laugh and he allowed that no nigger was a-going to look in no grave, 'cause he had tried to get me to go over there with him at night and I was scared.

One night, just as Doc was a-covering up, he heard them wooden shoes a-coming. So, he sat up in the grave and took his white shirt and put it over his head. He seed three shadows a-coming. Just as they got near the doc, the moon come out from behind a cloud and Doc, he wave that white shirt, and he say them niggers just fell over gravestones a-getting out of that graveyard. Doc allowed that he heard them wooden shoes a-going up the road for three miles. Well, they never did bother the doctor anymore.

HESTER HUNTER

Age 85, when interviewed by
Annie Ruth Davis, in Marion, S.C.;
May 1937.

Remember the first time them Yankees come. I was sitting down in the chimney corner and my mammy was giving me my breakfast. Remember I been sitting there with my milk and my bowl of hominy, and I hear my old grandmammy come a-running in from out the yard and say all the sky was blue as indigo with the Yankees coming right there over the hill. Say she see more Yankees than could ever cover up all the premises about there.

Then, I hear my missus scream and come a-running with a lapful of silver and tell my grandmammy to bury and sew that up in the feather bed, 'cause them Yankees was mighty apt to destroy all they valuables. Old Missus tell all the colored people to get away, get away and take care of themselves, and tell we children to get back to the chimney corner, 'cause she couldn't protect us noways, no longer.

I remember I hear tell that my old stepfather been gone to the mill to grind some corn, and when he was coming down the road, two big Yankees jump out the bushes side the road and tell him stop there. He say they tell him if he want to save his neck, he better get off that ox right then and get away from there. He say he been so scared he make for the woods fast as he could get there, and tell that he lay down with knots under his head many a night before he would venture to come out from that woods. Never hear tell of his ox and corn no more neither.

I remember my boss had one of my old missus' niggers up there in the yard one morning and say he was going whip him, and my missus say, "John C., you let my nigger alone." You see, my missus had her niggers and then Old Boss had his niggers, 'cause when Old Missus been marry Marster John C. Bethea, she had brought her share of niggers from where she was raised in the country.

It been like this, Old Missus' father had scratched the pen for every one of his chillun to have so many niggers apiece for they portion of his property, so long as they would look after them and treat them good. Then, if there been talk that them chillun never do what he say do, they was to take them niggers right back to they old marster home. But, child, they never didn't take no niggers away from my old missus, 'cause she sure took care of them. Stuck to her niggers till she died.

I remember just as good there been two long row of nigger house up in the quarter, and the Bethea niggers been stay in the row on one side, and the Davis niggers been stay in the row on the other side. And, honey, there been so much difference in the row on this side and the row on that side. My God, child, you could go through there and spot the Sara Davis niggers from the Bethea niggers time you see them.

All Old Missus' niggers had they brush pile side they house to sun they beds on and dry they washing, 'cause my missus would see to it herself that they never kept no nasty living. We was raise decent, honey, and that howcome me and my chillun is that way to this very day.

No, ma'am, ain't nobody never didn't turn no key on me. I remember, if my old missus would hear talk that we been bother something that didn't belong to us, she would whip us and say, "I'm not mad, but you chillun have got to grow up some day. You might have to suffer worse than this, if you don't learn better while you young."

Them niggers what been bred on Marster John C. Bethea's plantation never know nothing but big living in that day and time. Recollect that they would give all they colored people so much of flour for they Sunday eating, and then they had a certain woman on the place to cook all the other ration for the niggers in one big pot out in Old Marster's yard.

All the niggers would go there to the pot on Sunday and get they eating, like turnips and collards and meat, and carry it to they house and make they own bread. Then, in the weektime, they would come out the field at twelve o'clock and stand around the pot and eat they pan of ration, and then they would go back in the field and work.

When they would come home at night, there would be enough cooked up for them to carry home to last till the next day dinner. Didn't eat no breakfast no time. Had meat, greens, cornbread, and dumplings to eat mostly, and won't no end to milk.

Course, them what been stay to the white folks' house would eat to the missus' kitchen. And, my Lord, child, my white folks had the prettiest kind of rice that they made right there on they own plantation. Had plenty rice to last them from one year to the other, just like they had they hominy.

Then Old Marster had a big fish pond, and in the summertime when it would get too hot to work, he would allow all his plantation niggers to catch all the pikes and jacks they wanted and salt them down in barrels for the winter. Din't allow nobody to go nowhere about that fish pond but us niggers.

And another thing, they wouldn't cure they meat with nothing but this here green hickory wood, and I speak about what I been know, there ain't never been nothing could touch the taste of them hams and shoulder meat. Oo-oo-oo, honey, they would make the finest kind of sausages in them days. I tell my chillun I just about turn against these sausage the people make about here these days.

Oh, the people, they is awful worser than what they used to be. I know by my coming on that they awful worser. The little tots about here these days know things the older people used to be the only ones

that know about. I does worry about it so much.
Sometimes, child, I goes along just a-whistling,
"Lord, I wish I had went before I had so much
to grieve over."

BEN HORRY

Age 87, *when interviewed by*
Genevieve W. Chandler,
in Murrells Inlet, S.C.; August 1937.

I the oldest liver left on Waccamaw Neck, that belong
to Brookgreen, Prospect, Longwood, Alderly plantations. I been here! I seen thing! I tell you. That woods
you see been Colonel Josh Ward's taters patch. Right
to Brookgreen Plantation where I born.

They say Colonel Ward the biggest rice man been
on Waccamaw. He start that big gold rice in the country. He the head rice captain in them time. My father,
the head man, he tote the barn key. Rice been money,
them day and time.

My father love he liquor. That take money. He
ain't have money, but he have the rice barn key and
rice been money. So my father gone in woods, take a
old stump, have 'em hollow out. Now he same as
mortar [used for separating seed from husk] to the
barnyard. And my father keep a pestle hide handy.
Hide *two* pestle! Them pestle make outer heart pine.
When that pestle been missed, I wasn't know nothing.

The way I knows my age, when the slavery-time
war come, I been old enough to go in the woods with
my father and hold a lightwood torch for him to see to
pestle off that golden rice he been tote out the barn

and hide. *That* rice he been take to town Saturday when the Colonel and my father go to get provision, like sugar, coffee, pepper, and salt. With the money he get when he sell that rice, he buy liquor. He been hide that sack of rice before day clean, in the prow of the boat, and cover with a thing like an old coat.

I remembers one day when he come back from town he make a miss when he unloading and fell and broke he jug. The big boss see; he smell; and he see *why* my father make that miss step. He already sample that liquor. But the boss ain't say too much.

Saturday time come to ration off. Every head on the plantation to Brookgreen line up at smokehouse to draw he share of meat, rice, grits, and meal. (This was before my father been appointed head man. This when they had a tight colored man in that place by name Fraser. They say Fraser come straight from Africa.)

Well, Saturday, when time come to give my father he share of rations, the head man reach down in the corner and pull out a piece of that broke whiskey jug and put on top my father rations where all could see. Colonel Ward cause that to be done to broke him off from that whiskey jug. My father was a steady liquor man till then, and the boss broke him off.

Slavery going in. I remembers Marster Josh and Miss Bess had come from French Broad where they summered it. They brought a great deal of this cloth they call blue drilling to make a suit for every boy big enough to wear a suit of clothes and a pair of shoes for every one. I thought *that* the happiest setup I had in boyhood. Blue drilling pants and coat and shoe. And Sunday come, we have to go to the big house for Marster Josh to see how the clothes fit. And him and Miss Bess make us run races to see who run the fastest. That the happiest time I remembers when I was a boy to Brookgreen.

Two Yankee gunboats come up Waccamaw River. Come by us plantation. One stop to Sandy Island, Montarena Landing. One gone Wachesaw Landing. Old Marster Josh and all the white buckra [Gullah dialect for white person] gone to Marlboro County to hide from Yankee. Gone up Waccamaw River and up Pee Dee River, to Marlboro County, in a boat by name *Pilot Boy*. Take Colonel Ward and all the Captain to hide from gunboat till peace declared. I think *Pilot Boy* been a rear-wheeler. Most boats like the *Old Planter* been side-wheeler.

They say the Yankee broke in all the rice barn on Sandy Island and share the rice out to colored people. The big mill to Laurel Hill been burn right then. That the biggest rice mill on Waccamaw River. Twasn't the Yankee burn them mill. These white mens have a idea the Yankee mean to burn these mill so they set 'em afire before the Yankee come. Nothing left to Laurel Hill today but the rice mill tower. That old brick tower going to *be* there. Fire can't harm 'em.

The worst thing I remembers was the colored overseer. He was the one straight from Africa. He the boss over all the mens and womens, and if womans don't do all he say, he lay task on 'em they ain't able to do. My mother won't do all he say. When he say, "You go barn and stay till I come," she ain't do 'em. So, he have it in for my mother and lay task on 'em she ain't able for do.

Then, for punishment, my mother is take to the barn and strapped down on thing called The Pony. Hands spread like this and strapped to the floor and all two both she feet been tied like this. And she been give twenty-five to fifty lashes till the blood flow. And my father and me stand right there and look and ain't able to lift a hand! Blood on floor in that rice barn when barn tear down by Huntington.

If Marster Josh been know about that overseer, the overseer can't do em, but just the house servant get Marster Josh and Miss Bess ear. Them things different when my father been make the head man. What I tell you happen before Freedom, when I just can remember.

Father dead just before my mother. They stayed right to Brookgreen Plantation and dead there after they free. And all they chillun do the same, till the old colonel sell the plantation out. Where we going to? Ain't we got house and rations there?

After Freedom, from my behavior with my former owner, I was appointed head man on Brookgreen

Plantation. When canal been dug out from the Oaks Plantation to Dr. Wardie C. Flagg house, I was appointed head man. Canal cut 1877. Near as I can, I must task it on the canal and turn in every man's work to Big Boss. That canal bigger than one Mr. Huntington dig right now with machine.

More than one storm I live through. Been through the Flagg storm. Been turned over twice outside there in the sea. One time been have the seine. Been rough. Have weather. And the breakers take the boat. I swim till I get the rope hold. Two men on the shore have the rope end of the seine rope and I hold to that, and that how I save that time.

'Member another time. Had a boat full of people this last go-round. Was Miss Mary, her aunty, and lawyer. I take them fishing outside in ocean. Been in the inlet mouth. Come halfway to Drunken Jack Island. Breaker start to lick in the boat. I start to bail. Have a tomato can for bail with. And that been dangerous, have too much women in there; they couldn't swim like a man. And it happen by accident, when the boat swamp and full with water, our *feet touch bottom*. When he turn over, I didn't aim to do nothing but swim for myself. Wasn't able to help nobody. But here our feet touch bottom. Only an accident from God!

One time again I swamp outside, 'tween Georgetown and Charleston. Try to bail. Swim with one hand, hold boat with the other. Roughest time I ever

see 'cause it been cold weather. Old before-time yawl
boat, carry eight oar, four to each side. Young man
then—1877. After the weather surrender, we gone
back in there and find cork going up and down and
save us net and all.

When the Flagg storm been, 1893, I working for
Ravanel and Holmes. I was taken up in that storm in a
steamer boat. Leave Charleston generally about five in
morning. That trip never reach Georgetown till nine
that night. Meet a man on that trip got he wife hugged
to mast in a little kinder lifeboat. Had he two chillun,
rope wrap 'em to that mast. Save man and wife and
chillun, and gone back, and save he trunk. After that,
they quit call me Ben; they call me Rooster.

After Flagg storm, Colonel Ward take me and Peter
Carr, us two and a horse, take that shore to Little
River. Search for all them what been drowned. Find a
trunk to Myrtle Beach. Have all kinder thing in 'em:
comb for you hair, thing you put on you wrist. Find
dead horse, cow, ox, turkey, fowl—everything. Gra-
cious God! Don't want to see no more thing like that!
But no dead body find on beach outside Flagg family.

Find two of them chillun way down to Dick Pond
what drownded to Magnolia Beach, find them in a
distance apart from here to that house. All that family
drown out, because they wouldn't go to this lady
house on higher ground. Wouldn't let none of the
rest go. Servant all drown. Betsy, Kit, Mom Adele.
Couldn't identify who lost from who save till next

morning. Find old Doctor body by he vest stick out of the mud. Fetch Doctor body to shore and he watch still a-ticking. Dr. Wardie Flagg been save hanging to a beach cedar. When that tornado come, my house wash down off he blocks. Didn't broke up.

Religion? Reckon Stella [his wife] got the morest of that. I sometimes a little quick. Stella, she holds one course. I like good song. One I like best,

> Try us, Oh Lord,
> And search the ground
> Of every sinful heart!
> Whate'er of sin
> In us be found,
> Oh, bid it all depart!

Make my living with the oyster. Before time, I get seventy-five cents a bushel; now I satisfy with fifty cents. Tide going out, I go out in a boat with the tide. Tide bring me in with sometimes ten, sometimes fifteen or twenty bushels. I make white folks a roast. White folks come to Uncle Ben from all over the country—Florence, Dillon, Mullins—every kind of place. Same price roast or raw, fifty cents a bushel.

JAKE MCLEOD

Age 83, when interviewed by
Lucile Young and H. Grady Davis,
in Timmonsville, S.C.; August 1937

I born in Lynchburg, South Carolina the thirteenth day of November 1854. Born on the McLeod place. Grandparents born on the McLeod place, too. My white folks, they didn't sell and buy slaves; and that howcome my grandfather Riley McLeod fell to Frank McLeod and Grandmother fell to the McRaes.

My boss give my grandfather to his sister, Carolina, that had married the McRae, so they wouldn't be separated. They take them and go to Florida, and when the Yankees went to Florida, they hitched up the teams and offered to bring them back to South Carolina. Some of my uncles and aunts come back, but my grandfather and grandmother stayed in Florida till they died.

The McLeods, they was good people. Believe in plenty work, eat and wear all the time, but work us very reasonable. The overseer, he blow horn for us to go to work at sunrise. Give us task to do, and if you didn't do it, they put the little thing to you. That was a leather lash or some kind of a whip. Didn't have no whipping post in our neighborhood.

They didn't have no jails in them days, but I recollects one woman hanged on the galleries [gallows].

Hang them up by harness and broke neck for wrong-doing, like killing somebody or trying to kill. Old woman cooking for the Scotts, named Peggy, tried to poison the Scotts. Mean to her, she say, and she put poison in the coffee. My mother walked about ten miles to see that hanging, 'cause they turned the slaves loose to go to a hanging. Took her from the quarter in the wagon, and I heard her tell that the old lady, Peggy, was sitting on her coffin. My mother say she used to use so much witchcraft, and someone whispered, "Why don't you do something about it?" She say, "It too late now." I hear tell about them hanging, but I ain't see none of it.

My boss had four slave house that was three or four hundred yards from his house, and I reckon he had about twenty-five slaves. One was pole house with brick chimney, and two rooms partitioned off; and the other three was clay house. Us had frame bed and slept on shucks and hay mattress.

They didn't give us no money, but had plenty to eat every day. Give us buttermilk, sweet potatoes, meat, and cornbread to eat mostly. Catch a nigger with wheat, they give him "wheat." Then, they let us have a garden and extra patches of we own that we work on Saturday evenings. And we catch as much rabbits and fish as us want. Catch pikes and eels and cats. Catch fish with hook and line in Lynches River with Senator E. D. Smith's father. The Reverend Bill Smith the father of E. D. Smith.

The white folks, they had a woman to each place to weave the cloth and make all us clothes. The women had to weave five cuts a week, one cut a night. Have reel in the shape of wheel. Spoke turn and hold thread and turn and when it click, it a cut. Any over, keep it to the next week.

They wore cotton clothes in the summer and wool clothes in the winter, and had more than one garment, too. Had different clothes to wear on Sunday, 'cause the slaves go to the white folks' church in that day and time. Then, they had shoemaker to come there and make all the colored people's shoes. The Durant shoemaker come to the McLeod plantation and make they shoes.

I telling you my boss was a good man. He had a big plantation with six or seven hundred acres of land, but he didn't have to mind to see about none of the work. The overseer name Dennis, and he was the one to look out for all the plantation work. He lived on the McLeod place, and he was good man to us. I had to thin cotton and drop peas and corn, and I was a half-hand two years during the war. If a whole hand hoes one acre, then a half-hand hoes half a acre. That what a half-hand is.

Wheat, peas, corn, and cotton was the things that peoples plant mostly in them days. This how I see them frail the wheat out. Put pole in hard land and drive horse in circle and let them stamp it out. You could ride or walk. Two horses tramp and shake it out, and then take straws and have something to catch it in and wind it out. Had to pick and thrash a bushel of peas a day.

When corn-hauling time come, every plantation haul corn and put in circle in front of the barn. Have two piles and appoint two captains. They take sides and give corn shucking like that. Shuck corn and throw in front of door, and sometimes shuck corn all night. After they get through with the shucking, give big supper and march all around Old Marster's kitchen and house. Have tin pans, buckets, and canes for music and dance in front of the house in the road. Go to another place and help them shuck corn the next time, and so on that way.

My old missus and marster, they always look after they slaves when they get sick. Use herbs for they medicine. I used to know different herbs my mother would get. Boneset and life-everlasting make teas for fever and colds. When I was a boy, they used to carry them what have smallpox by the swamp and built a dirt house for them. Kept them there and somebody carried food to them. People used to have holes in they skin with that thing, and most of them died.

I hear tell about one man running away from Black Creek and going to Free State. Catch ride with people that used to travel to Charleston hauling cotton and things. He come back about fifteen years after the war and lived in that place adjoin to me. Come back with barrels and boxes of old secondhand clothes and accumulated right smart here. Talk good deal about how he associated with the whites. Don't know howcome he run away, but they didn't catch up with him till it was too late.

The community have man then called patroller [local slave patrol; also patteroller, pataroller, pattyroller, etc.], and they business was to catch them that run away. Say like you be authorized to look after my place, you catch them that slipped off to another man place. Couldn't leave off plantation to go to another place without you ask for a pass and have it on you.

White folks used to kill beef what they call "club beef." If you kill beef this week, you send this one and that one a piece till the beef all gone. White folks give me pass and tell me carry beef and deliver it. Next time, another man send us beef.

I run away one time. Somehow, the overseer know where I was. I recollects Old Missus had me tied to the tester bedstead, and she whip me till the whip broke. I see her getting another arm about full, and I tear loose and run away. I slip home on steps at my mother's house, looking down, playing with the cat, and look up in her face. She say, "You good-for-nothing, you get out of here and get to that barn and help them shuck corn."

I go, but I didn't go in, 'cause I keep a watch on her.

All I know about the war that bring Freedom was that the war was going on. I remember when they couldn't get coffee, sugar, or nothing like that. You know that was a tough time to think about; we couldn't get no salt. Cut up potatoes and parch to make coffee. Boil dirt out the smokehouse and put liquor in food. Eat pokeberry for greens. Then one day we hear gunfire in Charleston and Missus make miration [outcry].

I don't remember Freedom, but I know when we signed the contract, the Yankees give us to understand that we was free as our marster was. Couldn't write, just had to touch the pen. Ask us what name we wanted to go in.

We work on then, for one-third the crop the first year, with the boss furnishing everything. Soon as got little ahead, went to sharecropping.

I tell you, it been a pretty hard time to be up against. I own this here place, and my nephew live here with me. They give him government job with the understanding he help me. Get $24.80 a month and live off that. If carried out like the president want it carried out, it be better than slavery time. You know, some slaves got along mighty bad, 'cause most of the white people wasn't like our white folks.

ADELINE JACKSON

Age 88, when interviewed by
W. W. Dixon, in Winnsboro, S.C.

I was born four miles southwest of where I is now, on the other side of Woodward Station. I was a slave of Old Marster John Mobley, the richest man, the largest landowner, and with more niggers than any other white man in the county. He was the seventh son of the seventh son, so he allowed, and you know that's a sign of a big family, lots of cows, mules, horses, money, chillun, and everything that's worth having.

He had a good wife, too. This the way he got her, he say. She the daughter of Old Major Andy McLean, who got a body full of bullets in the Revolution. The Old Major didn't want Katie to marry Marster John. Marster John git on a mule and ride up in the night. Miss Katie runned out, jump up behind him, run away, and marry Marster John.

They had the same birthday, March 27, but Marster John two years older than Miss Katie. That day was looked to, same as Christmas, every year that come. Big times then, I tell you!

My missus had long hair, touching the floor and could dance, so Marster John said, with a glass of water on top of her head.

Marster John got religion and went all the way, like the jailer in the Bible. All the house joined with him and most of the slaves. It was Baptist, and he built a spanking good church building down the road, all out of his own money. The cemetery there yet. He called it Fellowship. Some fine tombstones in there yet. The finest cost two thousand dollars; that's his daughter Nancy's tomb. Marster John and my old missus buried in there.

When my youngest missus, name Marion Rebecca, married her second cousin, Marster Edward P. Mobley, I was give to her and went with them to the June place. It was called that because old Dr. June built it and sold it to Marster Ed. I nursed her first chillun: Edward, Moses Hill, John, and Katie.

It was a large, two-story frame house, with chimneys at each gable end. Marster Edward got to be as rich as Old Marster; he owned the June place, the Rochelle plantation, the Peay place, and the Roebuck place. Yes, sir, course us had overseers for so many slaves and plantations.

Slaves lived in quarters, a stretch of small houses off from the White House [often used in speaking of the master's house. Also Big House]. Patrollers often come to search for stray slaves, wouldn't take your word for it. They would search the house. If they catch one without a pass, they whipped him.

In course of time, I was took off the nursing and put to the field. I dropped cotton seed, hoed some, and picked cotton. I never learned to read or write.

At certain times we worked long and hard, and you had to be particular. The only whipping I got was for chopping down a good cornstalk near a stump in a new ground. When farm work was not pressing, we got all of Saturday to clean up around the houses, and wash and iron our clothes.

Marster Henry Gibson was our doctor. Yes, women in family way worked up to near the time, but guess Dr. Gibson knowed his business. Just before the time, they was took out and put in the carding and spinning rooms.

Marster never sold a slave, but swaps were made with kinpeople to advantage, slaves' wives and husbands sometimes. Marster Edward bought a slave in Tennessee just 'cause he could play the fiddle. Named him Tennessee Ike, and he played along with Ben Murray, another fiddler. Sometime all of us would be called up into the front yard to play and dance and sing for Miss Marion, the chillun, and visitors. Everything lively at Christmas time, dances with fiddles, patting, and stick rattling; but when I joined the church, I quit dancing.

I went to White Poplar Springs Church, the Baptist church my missus attended. We got most our outside news Sunday at church. The preacher was Mr. Cartledge. He allowed Miss Marion was the flower of his flock.

Our neighbors was the Peays, the Durhams, the Picketts, the Barbers, and Boulwares. All these folks kept a pack of hounds to run deer and foxes. I has eat many pieces of deer.

After the war, a man came along on a red horse; he was dressed in a blue uniform and told us we was free. The Yankees that I remembers was not gentlefolks. They stole everything they could take. The meanest thing I ever see was shoats they half killed, cut off the hams, and left the other parts quivering on the ground.

I married Mose Jackson, after Freedom, and had a boy, Henry. Last I heard, he was at Shelby, North Carolina. My missus was a good Christian woman. She give me a big supper when I was married.

I was much happier them days than now. Maybe it won't be so bad when I gets my old age pension.

ADELE FROST

Age 93, when interviewed by
Hattie Mobley, in Richland County, S.C.

I was born in Adams Run, South Carolina, January
21, 1844. My father name was Robert King, and my
mother was Minder King. My father was born in Adams Run, but my mother came from Spring Grove,
South Carolina. My master was kind to his slaves, and
his overseers was all Negroes. He had a large farm at
Parker's Ferry.

I was brought here at the age of twelve to be maid
for Mr. Mitchell, from who I didn't get any money,
but a place to stay and plenty of food and clothes. I
never gone to school in my life, and Marster nor Missus ever help me to read. I used to wear thin clothes in
hot weather and warm, comfortable ones in the winter. On Sunday I wear a old-time bonnet, armhole
apron, shoes, and stocking. My bed was the old-time
four-post with pavilion [canopy] hanging over the top.

On the plantation was a meeting house in which we
used to have meetings every Tuesday night, Wednesday night, and Thursday night. I used to attend the
white church. Dr. Jerico was the pastor. Colored people had no preacher, but they had leader. Every slave
go to church on Sunday, cause they didn't have any

work to do for Marster. My grandma used to teach the catechism and how to sing. I joined the church 'cause I wanted to be a Christian, and I think everybody should be.

Funerals was at night, and when ready to go to the graveyard, everybody would light a lightwood knot as torch while everybody sing. This is one of the songs we used to sing:

> Going to carry this body
> To the graveyard,
> Graveyard, don't you know me?
> To lay this body down.

We ain't had no doctor. Our missus and one of the slaves would attend to the sick.

The Yankees take three nights to march through. I was afraid of them and climbed into a tree. One call me down and say, "I am your friend." He give me a piece of money and I wasn't afraid no more.

After the war, I still work as a maid for Mr. Mitchell.

My husband was Daniel Frost. We didn't have no wedding, just married at the judge office. We had three chillun.

I move here [near Columbia] with my granddaughter, about ten year ago.

MILTON MARSHALL

Age 82, when interviewed by
G. L. Summer, in Newberry, S.C., RFD;
September 1937

I live in Newberry County, a few miles from town on Mr. Alan Johnstone's place. I rent and make a fair living. I have ten children now living and two dead. They is all on a farm. I was born in Union County, just across the Newberry line, near the Goshen Hill section. I was young when we moved to Newberry, and I have lived there nearly all my life. My father, Ned Worthy, was a slave of Frank Bynum's mother. My mother was Maria Worthy, who was a slave of Dr. Burton Maybin. She cooked for a long time for the Maybin family.

My grandfather was called Jack, and he was a nigger-driver. That was a nigger that had to oversee the slaves when the marster was away from home. He would call the cows like this: "Soo–ey, Soo–ey" or "Sook, Sook." He called his dogs by whistling. He had several dogs. There was many dogs on the farms, mostly hounds and bird dogs.

When grandpa died and was buried, his dogs would get out and bark and trail just like trailing a rabbit, and the trail always led to the graveyard. There they would stand by his grave and howl for a long time, with their heads up in the air.

The old folks made medicines from root herbs and tree barks. Herb tea was made to keep away fevers. Marster always called his big chaps up to the house in the mornings and made them drink chinaberry tea to keep worms from getting in them. Many of the slaves, and some old white people, too, thought there was witches in them days. They believed a witch could ride you and stop blood circulation.

Marster Burt Maybin owned sixty-eight slaves, and I was one, and is the only one now living. We had no money in slavery time, just got food and clothes for our work. But my marster was a good feeder, always had enough to eat. Every Sunday he would give each nigger a quart of flour extra for breakfast. Some of the marsters didn't give niggers much to eat, and they had to slip off and steal.

We had plenty of what was the rule for eating in them days. We had homemade molasses, peas, corn-bread, and home-raised meat sometimes. We killed rabbits and possums to eat, and sometimes went fishing and hunting.

Our clothes was made at home, spun and wove by the women folks. Copper straw and white cloth was used. Our shoes was made by a shoemaker in the neighborhood who was named Liles. They was made with wooden soles or bottoms. They tanned the leather or had it tanned in the neighborhood. It was tacked around the soles. It was rawhide leather, and the shoes had to be soaked in warm water and greased with tallow or meat skin so the shoes would slip on the feet.

All of us had to go to work at daylight and work till dark. They whipped us a little and they was strict about some things. Us chaps did not learn to read and write; that is why I can't read and write today. Marster wouldn't allow us to learn.

I was small in slavery time, and played with the white chaps. Once he saw me and some other chaps, white chaps, under a tree playing with letter blocks. They had the ABCs on them. Marster got awful mad and got off his horse and whipped me good.

Some of the slaves was whipped while they was tied to a stock. My marster was all right, but awful strict about two things: stealing and telling a lie. He sure whipped them if they was caught in them things.

We had to work all day Saturdays, but Marster wouldn't let anybody work on Sunday. Sometimes he would give the women part of Saturday afternoons so they could wash. He wouldn't allow fishing and hunting on Sundays either, unless it looked like rain and the fodder in the field had to be brought in. He always give us Christmas Day off, and we had lots of good eats then.

A stage that was drawn by two horses went past our place. It carried mail and people. When Marster wanted to send word to any people in the neighborhood, he sent it by somebody on a horse.

We had good white neighbors in slavery time. I remember the old corn shuckings, cotton-pickings, and logrollings. He would ask all the neighbors' hands in and they would come by crowds. I can remember them good.

I remember the grain was put in drains and the horses was made to tramp on it to get the seed out. Then, it was put in a house and poured in a big wooden fan machine, which fanned out the chaff. The machine was turned by two men.

They made molasses by taking the cane and squeezing out the juice in a big wooden machine. The machines now is different. They is made of cast.

The niggers didn't have a church on the plantation but was made to go to the white folks' church and set in back of the church. They had to get a pass to go to church same as any other place, or the patrollers would catch 'em and beat 'em.

After the war was over, the niggers built brush arbors for to hold meetings in. I sure remember the old brush arbor and the glorious times then, and how the niggers used to sing and pray and shout. I am a Baptist and we baptized in the creek after we dammed it up to hold water deep enough. Sometimes, we used a water-hole in the woods. I remember one old Baptist song, it went:

> Down to the water I be baptized,
>   for my Savior die:

> Down to the water,
>   the River of Jordan,
> Where my Savior baptized.

When Freedom come, the slaves was notified that a white man by the name Ben White would come to the plantation and make a speech to them. He said, "Now that you is free, you will be with your marster, and he is willing to give you one-third of what you make. You is free, and there will be no more whippings." Then Marster said, while he was crying, "You stay on with me, and I'll give you food and clothes and one-third of what you make."

After the war, the Ku Klux did bad in our neighborhood. They killed five or six niggers. I guess it was 'cause they was Republicans and had trouble at voting times.

I married Missouri Rice at her own house. We had a big wedding, and she wore a white dress with two frills on it. I wore a dove-colored suit and a high brim hat with a small crown. I bought the hat for seven dollars just to marry in, but used it for Sundays.

I never did think slavery was right. I was just a chap then and never thought much about it till long since it was over. I am a Democrat and always was one. I was forty years old when I repented of my sins and joined the church. I wanted to join and be baptized and be saved.

ALEXANDER SCAIFE

Age 82, when interviewed by
Caldwell Sims, in Pacolet, S.C. (Box 104)

Marster Charner Scaife a-laying on his bed of death is about the first thing that stuck in my mind. I felt sorry for everybody then. Miss Mary Rice Scaife, his wife, was mean. She died a year after. Never felt sad nor glad then, never felt no ways out of the regular way.

Overseers I recollects was: Mr. Sam Hughes, Mr. Tom Baldwin, and Mr. Whitfield Davis. Mr. Baldwin was the best to me. He had a still-house out in a field where liquor was made. I tote it for him. We made good corn liquor. Once a week I brung a gallon to the big house to Marster. Once I got happy offen it, and when I got there, lots of it was gone. He had me whipped. That the last time I ever got happy offen Marster's jug.

When I was a shaver, I carried water to the rooms and polished shoes for all the white folks in the house. Set the freshly polished shoes at the door of the bedroom. Get a nickel for that and dance for joy over it.

Two big gals cleaned the rooms up. I helped carry out things, take up ashes, fetch wood, and build fires early every day. Marster's house had five bedrooms and a setting room. The kitchen and dining room was in the back yard. A covered passage kept them from getting wet when they went to the dining room. Marster said he had rather get cold going to eat than to have the food get cold while it was being fetched to him. So, he had the kitchen and dining room joined, but most folks had the dining room in the big house.

It took a week to take the cotton boat from Chester to Columbia. Six slaves handled the flatboat: the boatman, two oarsmen, two steermen, and an extra man. The steermen was just behind the boatman. They steered with long poles on the way up the river and paddled down the river. The two oarsmen was behind them. They used to pole, too, going up, and paddle going down.

Seventy-five or eighty bales was carried at a time. They weighed around three hundred pounds apiece. In Columbia, the wharfs was on the Congaree banks. For the cotton, we got all kinds of supplies to carry home. The boat was loaded with sugar and coffee coming back. On the Broad River, we passed by Woods Ferry, Fish Dam Ferry, Henderson's Ferry, Henderson's Island, and some others, but that is all I recollect. We unloaded at our own ferry called Scaife Ferry.

ZACK HERNDON

Age 93, when interviewed by
Caldwell Sims, in Gaffney, S.C.,
Grenard Street; May 1937.

Yes, sir, my old marster had lots of land, a big plantation down at Lockhart where I was born, called the Herndon Plantation. Then he live in a big house just outside of Union, called Herndon Terrace, and besides that, he was the biggest lawyer that was in Union.

First remembrance was at the age of three when as yet I couldn't walk none. My mother cooked some gingerbread. She told the chilluns to go down a hill and get her some oak bark. The first one back with the bark would get the first gingerbread cake that was done.

My sister sat me down, a-sliding down the side of her leg, after she had carried me with her down the side of the hill. Them big chaps started to fooling time away. I grab up some bark in my hand and went toddling and a-crawling up to the house. My mother seed me a-crawling and toddling, and she took the bark out of my hand and let me pull up to the door. She cook the gingerbread, and when the other chilluns got back, I was a-setting up eating the first cake.

She put gingerbread dough in a round oven that had legs on it. It looked like a skillet, but it never had no handle. It had a lid to go on the top with a groove to hold live coals. Live coals went under it, too. Mother wanted oak chips and bark, 'cause they made such good hot coals and clean ashes.

Pots boiled in the back of the chimney, a-hanging from a pot rack over the blazing fire. It had pot hooks to get it down.

Bread was cooked in a baker, like the ginger cake was. They roasted both kinds of taters in the ashes and made cornbread in the ashes and called it ash cake, then.

Us lived in a one-room log house. For the larger families, they had two rooms with the fireplace in the middle of the room. Ours was at the end by the window. It had white or red oak, or pine shingles to cover the roof with. Of course, the shingles was handmade, never knowed how to make no others.

All beds was corded. Alongside the railings, there was holes bored to draw the ropes through, as these was what they used in them days instead of slats. Ropes could be stretched to make the bed lay good. Us never had a chair in the house. My pa made benches for us to sit by the fire on. Marster Zack let the overseer get planks for us.

My pa was called Lyles Herndon. We had a large plank table that Pa made. Never had no mirrors. Went to the spring to see ourselves on a Sunday morning. Never had no such things as dressers in them days. All us had was a table, benches, and beds. And my pa made them. Had plenty wood for fire and pine knots for lights when the fire get low or stop blazing.

Us had tallow candles. Why, everybody knowed how to make tallow candles in them days, that wasn't nothing out of the ordinary. All you had to do was to kill a beef and take the tallow from his tripe and kidneys. See, it the fat you get and boil it out, stew it down just as folks does hog lard these days.

The candle moulds was made out of tin. For the wicks, all the wrapping string was saved up, and there wasn't much wrapping string in them times. Put the string right down the middle of the mould and pour the hot tallow all around it. The string will be the wick for the candle. Then the moulds was laid in real cold water so that the tallow shrink when it harden, and this allow the candle to drop easy from the mould and not break up. Why, it's just as easy to make tallow candles as it is to fall off a log.

Marster Zack had a hundred slaves on that plantation. Stout, healthy ones brung from one thousand dollars on up to two thousand dollars a head. When I was a young kid, I heard that he was offered eight hundred for me, but he never took it.

Marster Zack never bred no slaves, but us heard of such afar off. He let his darkies marry when they wanted to. He was a good man. He always allowed the slaves to marry as they pleased, 'cause he allowed that

God never intent for no souls to be bred as if they was cattle. And he never practice no such.

After Mr. Herndon died, I was sold at the sale at Lockhart, to Dr. Tom Bates from Santuc. He bought me for eighteen hundred dollars, so as they always told me. This the onliest time that I was ever sold.

First lamp that I ever seed was a tin lamp. It was a little table lamp with a handle and a flat wick. That was at Dr. Bates's place in Santuc. He had it in his house. Him and his brother lived together. Dr. Bates's brother, Fair, was single man that live in the house with Dr. Bates for thirteen years. I was Dr. Bates's houseboy.

As houseboy there, I mind the flies from the table and tote dishes to and fro from the kitchen. Kitchen far ways off from the house. James Bates, his cook. Sometime I help wash the dishes. Marster never had no big house, 'cause he was late marrying. There wasn't no company in them days, neither.

Rations was give out every week from the smokehouse. On Saturday, us get one peck meal, three pounds of meat, and one-half gallon black molasses for a person. That's lot more than they gets in these days and times. Sunday morning us get two, or maybe, three pounds of flour. Didn't know nothing about no fatback in them times. Had sassafras, sage teas, and dinty tea [a tea brewed from a South Carolina weed].

Twenty-five or thirty hogs was killed at the time. Lots of sheep and goats was also killed. All our meat was raised, and us wore wooden-bottom shoes. Raised all the wheat and corn. Hogs, cows, goats, and sheep just run wild on Tinker and Brushy Fork creeks.

Never seed no ice in them days 'cept in winter. Summertime, things was kept in the milk-house. Well water was changed every day to keep things cool. Everybody drink milk in the summer, and leave off hot tea, and the white folks only drink coffee for their breakfast.

Marster's saddle horse was kinder reddish. Generally, he do his practice on horseback. He good doctor, and carry his medicine in saddle bags. It was leather and fall on each side of the horse's side. When you put something in it, you have to keep it balanced. Don't never see no saddle bags, neither does you see no doctors going round on no horses, these days.

I lived in slavery for over twenty-one years. Yes, I's twenty-one when Freedom come. Then Dr. Bates up and marry Mr. Henry Sartor's daughter, Miss Mary. Don't know how long she live, but she up and took and died. Then he pop up and marry her sister, Anne. It was already done Freedom when he marry the first time. When he married the second time, Mr. Fair up and went over to the Keenan place to live. He never did marry, hisself, though.

My son took me back to Union last year, 1936. Nothing didn't look natural, 'cept the jail. Everything else look strange. Didn't see nobody I knowed, not nary living soul. Marster's big white house, with them columns, still setting there, but the front all growed up in pine trees. When I slave-time darky, that front had flowers and figures setting all along the drive from the road to the big house. Tain't like that now.

ADELINE JOHNSON

Age 93, when interviewed by
W.W. Dixon in Winnsboro, S.C.

I born on what is now called the Jesse Gladden place, but it all belong to my old marster, William Hall, then.

My old marster was one of the richest men in the world. Him have lands in Chester and Fairfield counties, Georgia and Florida, and one place on the Red River in Arkansas. He also had a plantation to raise brown sugar on, in old Louisiana. Then him and his brother Daniel built and give Bethesda Church, that's standing yet, to the white Methodists of Mitford, for them to attend and worship at. He remembered the Lord, you see, in all his ways and the Lord guide his steps.

I never have to do no field work, just stayed round the house and wait on the missus, and the chillun. I was whipped just one time. That was for marking the mantelpiece with a dead coal of fire. They make Mammy do the lashing. Hadn't hit me three licks before Miss Dorcas, Miss Jemima, Miss Julia, and Marster Johnnie run there, catch the switch, and say, "That enough, Mama Ann! Addie won't do it again." That's all the beating I ever received in slavery time.

I was about raised up in the house. In the evening, I fill them boxes with chips and fat splinters. When morning come, I go in there and make a fire for my young missuses to get up by. I help dress them and comb their hair. Then, I goes downstairs and put flowers on the breakfast table and lay the Bible by Marster William's chair. Then I bring in the breakfast. Table have to be set the night before. When everything was on the table, I ring the bell. White folks come down, and I wait on the table.

After the meal finish, Marster William read the Bible and pray. I clear the table and help wash the dishes. When that finish, I cleans up the rooms. Then, I acts as maid and waitress at dinner and supper. I warms up the girls' room, where they sleep, after supper. Then go home to Poppy John and Mama Ann. That was a happy time, with happy days.

The white folks near was the Mellichamps, the Gladdens, the Mobleys, Lumpkins, Boulwares, Fords, Picketts, and Johnsons.

After Freedom I marry a preacher, Tom Johnson. Him die when in his sixties, thirty years ago. I hope and prays to get to heaven. I'll be satisfied to see my Savior that my old marster worshipped and my husband preach about. I want to be in heaven with all my white folks, just to wait on them, and love them, and serve them, sorta like I did in slavery time. That will be enough heaven for Adeline.

REBECCA JANE GRANT

Age 92, when interviewed by
Phoebe Faucette, in Lena, S.C.

I was just a little girl, about eight years old, staying in
Beaufort at the missus' house, polishing her brass and-
irons and scrubbing her floors, when one morning she
say to me, "Janie, take this note down to Mr. Wilcox
Wholesale Store on Bay Street and fetch me back the
package the clerk give you."

I took the note. The man read it, and he say, "Uh-
huh." Then he turn away and he come back with a
little package, which I took back to the missus.

She open it when I bring it in and say, "Go upstairs,
Miss!"

It was a raw cowhide strap about two feet long, and
she started to pouring it on me all the way upstairs. I
didn't know what she was whipping me about, but she
pour it on, and she pour it on.

Directly, she say, "You can't say 'Marster Henry,'
Miss? You can't say 'Marster Henry?'"

"Yes'm. Yes'm. I can say 'Marster Henry!'"

Marster Henry was just a little boy about three or
four years old. Come about halfway up to me. Wanted me to say "Marster" to him—a baby!

My mother and four of us children were sold to Mr.
Robert Oswald in Beaufort. My father belong to Mar-

ster Tom Willingham, but my mother belong to another white man. Marster Tom was always trying to buy us so we could all be together, but the man wouldn't sell us to him. We had to leave all the folks we know when we was took to Beaufort.

All of us chillun, too little to work, used to have to stay at the "Street" [slave quarters]. They'd have some old folks to look after us—some old man or some old woman. They'd clean off a place on the ground near the washpot where they cooked the peas, clean it off real clean, then pile the peas out there on the ground for us to eat. We'd pick 'em up in our hands and begin to eat.

Sometimes, they'd cook hoecakes in a fire of coals. They'd mix a little water with the meal and make a stiff dough that could be patted into shape with the hands. The cakes would be put right into the fire and would be washed off clean after they were raked out from the coals.

My mother say she didn't know a soul. All the time she'd be praying to the Lord. She'd take us chillun to the woods to pick up firewood, and we'd turn around to see her down on her knees behind a stump, a-praying. We'd see her wiping her eyes with the corner of her apron, first one eye, then the other, as we come along back. Then, back in the house, down on her knees, she'd be a-praying. One night she say she been down on her knees a-praying and that when she got up, she looked out the door and there she saw coming down out the elements a man, pure white and shining.

He got right before her door, and come and stand right to her feet, and say, "Sarah, Sarah, Sarah. You're not parted from your husband. You're just over a little slash of water. Who do you put your trust in?"

My mother say, after that, everything just flow along, just as easy. Now my mother was an unusually good washer and ironer. The white folks had been saying, "Wonder who it is that's making the clothes look so good?" Well, about this time, they found out; and they would come bringing her plenty of washing to do. And when they would come, they would bring her a pan full of food for us chilluns.

Soon the other white folks from round about heard of her, and she was getting all the washing she needed. She would wash for the missus during the day, and for the other folks at night. And they all was good to her.

One day the missus call her to the house to read her something from a letter she got. The letter say that my father had married another woman. My mother was so upset she say, "I hope he breaks that woman's jawbone. She know she ain't his lawful wife." And they say her wish come true. That was just what happened.

They used to make the clothes for the slaves in the house. Had a seamstress to stay there in the house so the missus could supervise the work. The cloth the clothes was made out of was handwoven. It was dyed in pretty colors—some green, some blue, and pretty colors. And it was strong cloth, too. Times got so hard during the war that the white folks had to use the cloth woven by hand, themselves.

The ladies would wear bustles, and hoops made out of oak. Old times, they'd make underbodies with whalebone in it. There was something they'd put over the hoop they call "follow me, boy." Used to wear the skirts long, with them long trains that trail behind you. You'd take and tuck it up behind on some little hook or something they had to fasten it up to. And the little babes had long dresses. Come down to your feet when you hold the baby in your lap. And embroidered from the bottom of the skirt all the way up. Oh, they were embroidered up in the finest sort of embroidery.

Didn't have no colored churches. The drivers and the overseers, the house-servants, the bricklayers, and folks like that'd go to the white folks' church. But not the field hands. Why, they couldn't have all got in the church. My marster had three or four hundred slaves, himself. And most of the other white folks had just as many or more. But them as went would *sing*. Oh, they'd sing! I remember two of them specially. One was a man and he'd sing bass. Oh, he'd roll it down! The other was a woman, and she'd sing soprano. They had colored preachers to preach to the field hands down in the quarters. They'd preach in the street. Meet next day to the marster's and turn in the report. How many pray, how many ready for baptism, and all like that.

Used to have Sabbath school in the white people's house, on the porch, on Sunday evening. The porch was big and they'd fill that porch. They never fail to give the chillun Sabbath school. Learn them the Sabbath catechism. And they was taught they must be faithful to the missus and marster's work like you would to your heavenly Father's work.

We'd sing a song the church bells used to ring in Beaufort. You never hear it anymore. But I remembers it:

> I want to be an angel, and with an
>   angel stand,
> A crown upon my forehead, a harp
>   within my hand.
> Right there before my Savior, so
>   glorious and so bright,
> I'll hear the sweetest music, and
>   praise Him day and night.

At the white folks' church at Lawtonville, they had a colored man who used to sing for them by the name of Moses Murray. He'd sit there back of the organ and roll down on them bass. Roll down just like the organ roll! He was Moses Lawton at that time, you know.

I was fifteen years old when I left Beaufort, at the time Freedom was declared. We were all reunited then. First, my mother and the young chillun, then I got back. My uncle, Jose Jenkins, come to

Beaufort and stole me by night from my missus. He took me with him to his home in Savannah. We had been done freed, but he stole me away from the house.

When my father heard that I wasn't with the others, he sent my grandfather, Isaac, to hunt me. When he find me at my uncle's house, he took me back. We walked back—all sixty-four miles. I was foundered. You know, if a foundered person will jump over a stick of burning lightwood, it will make 'em feel better.

You know how old I am? I'm in my ninety-fourth year. Ella has a dream book she looks up my age in and tells me what luck I have, and all that. I generally had good luck.

Mrs. Green Grinding Corn, 1907

From the Penn School Collection
Courtesy of the Penn Center, Inc., St. Helena Island, South Carolina

Courtesy of the Library of Congress

Courtesy of South Caroliniana Library,
University of South Carolina

Baptism, Ebenezer Church, October 1910
From the Penn School Collection
Courtesy of the Penn Center, Inc., St. Helena Island, South Carolina

Returning from the Fields
Courtesy of The New-York Historical Society, New York

Bringing Home Firewood
From the Penn School Collection
Courtesy of the Penn Center, Inc., St. Helena Island, South Carolina

Thaddeus Watkins at Home
From the Penn School Collection
Courtesy of the Penn Center, Inc., St. Helena Island, South Carolina

Island Home after a Storm
From the Penn School Collection
Courtesy of the Penn Center, Inc., St. Helena Island, South Carolina

Mrs. Green Winnowing her Rice
From the Penn School Collection
Courtesy of the Penn Center, Inc.,
St. Helena Island, South Carolina

From the Manigault Papers
Courtesy of the Southern Historical Collection,
University of North Carolina at Chapel Hill

ELIJAH GREEN

Age 94, when interviewed by
Augustus Ladson, at 156 Elizabeth Street,
Charleston, S.C.

From the southeast of Calhoun Street, which was then Boundary Street, to the Battery was the city limit. And from the northwest of Boundary Street for several miles was nothing but farm land. All my brothers was farm hands for our marster, George W. Jones. I was born in Charleston at 82 King Street, December 25, 1843. The house is still there who recent owner is Judge Whaley. My ma and pa was Kate and John Green.

I did all the housework till the war, when I was given to Mr. George W. Jones's son, William, as his "daily give" [a valet] servant who duty was to clean his boots, shoes, sword, and make his coffee. He was First Lieutenant of the South Carolina Company Regiment.

Being his servant, I wear all his cast-off clothes, which I was glad to have. My shoes was called brogan, that had brass on the toe. When a slave had one of them, you couldn't tell them he wasn't dressed to death.

As the daily give servant of Mr. William H. Jones, I had to go to Virginia during the war. In the battle at

Richmond, General Lee had General Grant almost beaten. When General Sherman got to Virginia, the battle was renewed and continued for seven days, at the end of which General Lee surrender to General Grant.

During the seven days' fight, the battle got so hot till Mr. William Jones made his escape, and it was two days before I know he was gone. One of the generals sent me home, and I got here two days before Mr. William got home. He went up in the attic and stay there till the war was end. I carry all his meals to him and tell him all the news. Marster sure was a frightened man; I was sorry for him. That battle at Richmond, Virginia, was the worst in American history.

Mr. Ryan had a private jail on Queen Street near the Planters' Hotel. He was very cruel; he'd lick his slaves to death. Very seldom one of his slaves survive a whipping. He was the opposite to Governor Aiken, who live on the northwest corner of Elizabeth and Judith streets. He had several rice plantations, hundreds of his slaves he didn't know.

Not till John C. Calhoun's body was carried down Boundary Street was the name changed in his honor. He is buried in St. Phillip's Churchyard, across the street, with a laurel tree planted at his head. Four men and me dig his grave, and I cleared the spot where his monument now stand. The monument was put up by Pat Collington, a Charleston mason. I never did like

Calhoun, 'cause he hated the Negro. No man was ever hated as much as him by a group of people.

The Work House (Sugar House) was on Magazine Street, built by Mr. Columbus G. Trumbone. On Charlmer [Chalmers] Street is the slave market from which slaves was taken to Vangue Range and auctioned off. At the foot of Lawrence Street, opposite East Bay Street, on the other side of the trolley tracks is where Mr. Alonzo White kept and sell slaves from his kitchen. He was a slave broker who had a house that extended almost to the train tracks, which is about three hundred yards going to the waterfront. No train or trolley tracks was there then, cause there was only one railroad here, the Southern, and the depot was on Ann Street, where the Bagging Mill now is.

When slaves run away and their marsters catch them, to the stockade they go, where they'd be whipped every other week for a number of months. And for God's sake, don't let a slave be catch with pencil and paper. That was a major crime. You might as well had killed your marster or missus.

One song I know I used to sing to the slaves when marster went away, but I wouldn't be so fool as to let him hear me. What I can remember of it is:

> Marster gone away,
> But darkies stay at home,
> The year of jubilee is come,
> And Freedom will begun.

The first two people that was hung in Charleston was Harry and Janie, husband and wife who was slaves of Mr. Christopher Black. Mr. Black had them whipped and they planned to kill the whole family. They poisoned the breakfast one morning, and if two of the family hadn't oversleep, they too would a-been dead. The others die almost instantly. An investigation was made and the poison discovered, and the two slaves hung on the big oak tree in the middle of Ashley Avenue.

When any in your owner's family was going to be married, the slaves was dressed in linen clothes to witness the ceremony. Only special slaves was chosen to be at the wedding. Slaves was always asked how they like the one who was coming in the family. I didn't like that, 'cause I had to lie on myself by saying nice things about the person and hate the person at the same time.

Slaves was always buried in the night, as no one could stop to do it in the day. Old boards was used to make the coffin that was blackened with shoe polish.

Mr. Stiles Bee, on James Island, give tract of land to the Negroes for a school just after the war. He put up a shed-like building with a few chairs in it. It was at the place called Cut Bridge.

After the war I did garden work. I was janitor at Benedict College in Columbia for two years and at Claflin in Orangeburg for twelve. Now all that is past, and I'm living from hand to mouth. The banks took all my money and I can't work or do the collecting for my landlord, and he give me a room free. If it wasn't for that, I don't know what I'd do.

AMY PERRY

*Age 82, when interviewed by
Jessie A. Butler, at 21 Pitt Street,
Charleston, S.C.; May 1937.*

 W e is live in the country, near Orangeburg, and I
remembers very little about the war and the time before the war. The colored people make they own cloth
and call 'em cotton osnaburg. They make banyans for
the chillun. Sleeve been cut in the cloth, and they
draw it up at the neck, and call 'em banyan [from the
body garment worn by *banians*, or Indian traders, in
West Africa]. They ain't know nothing about drawers
nor nothing like that.

The medicine I remember was castor oil, and dogwood and cherry bark, which they put in whiskey and
give you. They is give you this to keep your blood
good. Dogwood will bitter your blood; it good medicine, I know.

I remember the people have to get ticket for go out
at night. When they is gone to prayer meeting, I is see
them drag bush back of them, to outen they step
[obliterate footprints]. If the patrol catch you without
ticket, they beat you.

I remembers when the Yankee come through and
Wheeler army come after us. Those been dreadful
times. The Yankees massacred the people, burned

their houses, and stole the meat and everything they could find. The white folks have to live wherever they can, and they didn't have enough to eat. I know whole families live on one goose a week, cooked in greens. Sometimes they have punkin and corn, red corn at that. Times was hard, hard. The colored people didn't have nothing to eat neither. That why my aunty bring me to Charleston to live.

The first year after Freedom, I gone to school on Mr. John Townsend place, down to Rockville. After peace declared, the colored people lived on cornmeal mush and salt water in the week, and mush and vinegar for Sunday. Mind you, that for Sunday! I don't see how we live, yet we is.

About eight year after the war, we used to go down to the dairy for clabber. They give you so much for each one in the family—two tablespoon full for the grown people and one tablespoon for the chilluns. We add water to that and make a meal. In the country, the colored people live on a third [one-third of the season's crop], but, of course, at the end of the year, they didn't have nothing. Yet, they has lived.

Some people believe in dreams, but I don't have no faith in them. Lot of people believe in root and such, but they can't scare me with root. I roll over them from here to Jericho and they wouldn't bother me. A man died bad right in that house yonder. I went with the doctor, close his sight, and such; and I come right home, gone to bed, and sleep. He ain't bother me and

I ain't see him since. I don't believe in ghosts, nor dreams, nor conjure, that the worst.

Some people say they can see ghost, but you can't see ghost and live. I don't believe in 'um, no ghost, and no conjure, though my Uncle Cotton Judson and my Aunt Massie both believe in them. Uncle Cotton could do most as much as the devil he-self; he could most fly, but I never believe in 'um, no matter what he can do.

As long as old people live, they going to tell the young ones about ghost and thing. They going to pass it on. And when they die, they going to leave that foolishness right here. No, I don't believe in no conjure and no root. If they give me poison, then they got me.

You can eat your stomach full, and you'll dream. I believe in some kind of vision. You doze off, and you have a good dream. I believe that. People get converted in dreams. I was twelve year old when I get converted. I dreamed I was in a field, a large green field. A girl was there that I didn't had no use for. I had a bundle on my back. I honey the girl up and love 'um and the bundle fall on the ground. They put me in the church then.

WILLIS WILLIAMS

Age 89/90, when interviewed by
Genevieve W. Chandler,
in Conway, S.C.; May 1935.

When I was born, been August. I was a man grown pulling boxes [turpentine boxes] when the shake was [the 1886 earthquake]. I know the very night the shake come—on a Wednesday night. I was on doorstep, loosing my shoestring. There was more religion then than they is now. Praying and prayer meeting for a month. Everybody tend meeting.

The man I belonged to been Marster John A. Williams, born on the Cape Fear. I goes by Marster John name—Williams.

Marster John Williams had four hundred slaves. He was a man *had* the colored people. He didn't work all on his own plantation. He'd hire out his people to work turpentine—put 'em out for so much a year. He'd give 'em blanket, suit, coat, pants. First of the year come, Boss would collect wages for all he hire out.

When I was houseboy for old Marster John, waiting on white people, that was the best and easiest time I ever had. Ever Saturday, drive Marster John to Fayetteville. Ever Saturday, they'd think that store belong to me. I'd eat lumps of brown sugar out the barrel, candy, crackers. Did as I please then, *now* do as I can.

Remember when the Yankees come. Been Sunday morning. Ride up to the gate on horses. Old Boss happened to come out and walk to the lot. I happened to be at gate. They took his watch out his pocket, his pistol—had it girded to him—and took all he whiskey and catch chickens and guinea and take them all. Then, they gone in the lot and took two breeding mares and hitch them in wagon and loaded wagon full of corn. Then, they took the two carriage horses and hitched to carriage, gone to smokehouse, and fill that carriage full of all Marster John sides of meat and ham and shoulders.

I been following and watching to see what all they going to take, and a soldier looked at me and say, "Come on, little nigger! Wanter go?"

And I done like another fool. I rode off behind the two brood mares, on the corn, and where they rested that night, I rested right there.

It was mighty cold up there. I suffered a heap in the cold before I got back home. They give me a horse—saddled and bridled—and a little bayonet gun. Put me on that horse to drive cattle. Tell me to take all I see. Didn't except *nobody* cattle. Night come, put 'em in pasture—put 'em in *anybody* field—on the oats, rye, wheat.

Sometimes, rain sure fall. Had to tend that bunch of cattle, rain or no rain. Didn't kill one beef and stop. *Four* beeves a day. Go out, get the hog, and kill 'em. Skin 'em. Didn't scald 'em and clean 'em like we do.

Just eat the ham. Rest throw away. Gone to Wilmington, Fayetteville, Rockfish, and Beaver Creek.

General Sherman? I *seen* him. He had a big name, but he warn't such a big man. He was a little spare-made man. I remember now when I seed him the last time. He had two matched horses going down to Petersburg. Six guards riding by the side of his turn-out. Oh my God, what clothes he had on! He was dressed down in finest uniform.

I remember it was Sunday morning that General Johnson throwed up his hand at Raleigh. Done with the war.

When I leave the Yankee, they give me thirty-five dollars in money. I been so fool, had never seen no greenback. Throwed it away eating crackers and peanuts. And I bought some brogan shoes. If I'd a helt on to that, I'd a-been somebody today.

Before Freedom, I have a good enough time. Just lay round the house and wait on my boss. When Freedom come and I did have to get out and work, it most kill me.

After Freedom, my mother wash for family to Beaver Creek. And after Freedom, my father went to working on shares. Old Marster John called 'em up and tell 'em, "You free, Asa. You free, Lewis. You free, Handy. You free, Wash. You can do as you please. You have to fadge for yourself now."

That there my second wife. How many wife I had? Two or three. Lemme see—[looking at present wife], you is one. You the last one. First one been Jinny Lind. Next one been Mary Dickson. And Caressa Pyatt been one. And there been another one. I forgot that woman name. Got it in my mouth and can't call it. I'll call the name of them others I take up with in a little while. One was Caroline; one was Tisha. I take them a little while; and if they didn't do to suit me, I put 'em out. Some I didn't stay with long enough to find out they name. Jinny Lind sister was Tisha. Jinny Lind gone, try her sister. Just a make-out. If they didn't do to suit me, I'd give 'em the devil and put 'em out.

> Woman, dog, cypress knee,
> More you beat em, the better they be!

But some woman, the more you beat 'em, the worse the devil gets in 'em. Get so they won't "gee" nor "haw." "Ways of woman and ways of snake deeper than the sea." I take that to mean mighty few can tell by the trail of a snake whether it's coming or going.

I hear story about the rabbit and the fox—all them old things—some times my mind franzy [fuzzy]. Been break up too much. Break two ribs to the lumber mill. Jump out a cart one day and run a ten-penny nail through my foot. That lay me up two months. Some mean people catch me up by that tree yonder with a car, and that lay me up sixty-five days. They pick me up for dead that time. All that make my mind get franzy sometimes. Come and go. Come and go.

SAM POLITE

Age 93, when interviewed by
Chlotilde R. Martin, in Beaufort County, S.C.

When gun shoot on Bay Point for Freedom, I been seventeen-year-old working slave. I born on B. Fripp Plantation, on St. Helena Island. My father belong to Mr. Marion Fripp, and my mother belong to Mr. Old B. Fripp. I don't know how mucher land, neither how much slave he have, but he have two big plantation and many slave—more'n a hundred slave.

Slave live on street—two row of house with two room to the house. My father and mother ain't marry. Slave don't marry; they just live together. All slave have for stay on plantation in daytime, but when work done, can visit wife on other plantation. Have pass, so patrol won't get 'um.

When I been little boy, I play on street—shoot marble, play army, and such thing. When horn blow and morning star rise, slave have for get up and cook. When day clean [after sunrise], they gone to field. Woman too old for work in field have for stay on street and mind baby. Old mens follow cow. Chillun don't work in field till twelve or thirteen year old. You carry dinner to field in your can and leave 'um at the heading [top of row]. When you feel hungry, you eat.

Every slave have task [quarter acre] to do, sometime one task, sometime two task, and sometime three. You have for work till task through. When cotton done make, you have other task. Have to cut cord of marsh grass maybe. Task of marsh been eight feet long and four feet high. Then, sometime you have to roll cord of mud in cowpen. Woman have to rake leaf from wood into cowpen.

When you knock off work, you can work on your land. Maybe you might have two or three task of land round your cabin what Marster give you for plant. You can have chicken, maybe hog. You can sell egg and chicken to store and Marster will buy your hog. In that way, slave can have money for buy thing like fish and whatever he want. We don't get much fish in slavery, 'cause we never have boat. But sometime you can throw out net and catch shrimp. You can also catch possum and raccoon with your dog.

On Saturday night, every slave that works gets peck of corn and pea, and sometime meat and clabber. You never see any sugar, neither coffee, in slavery. You has straw in your mattress, but they give you blanket. Every year, in Christmas month, you gets four or either five yard cloth, according to how you is. Out of that, you have to make your clote [clothes]. You wears that same clote till the next year. You wear it winter and summer, Sunday and every day. You don't get no coat, but they give you shoe.

In slavery, you don't know nothing about sheets for your bed. Us never know nothing about Santa Claus till Freedom, but on Christmas, Marster give you meat and syrup and maybe three day without work.

Slave work till dark on Saturday just like any other day. I still does work till dark on Saturday. But on Sunday, slave don't work. On Fourth of July, slave work till twelve o'clock and then knocks off. On Sunday, slave can visit back and forth on the plantations.

Slave don't do mucher frolic. When woman have baby, he [Gullah speech often substitutes masculine for other pronouns, including possessives] have midwife for nine day and sometime don't have to work for month when baby born. Missus send clote from Big House. When nigger sick, Marster send doctor. If you been very sick, doctor give you calomus or castor oil. Sometime he give you Dead-Shot for worms, or Puke [a powder] to make you heave. If I just have a pain in my stomach, my mother give me Jusee-e-moke [Jerusalem artichoke], what he get out of the wood.

If slave don't do task, they get licking with lash on naked back. Driver nigger give licking, but Marster most always been there. Sometime maybe nigger steal hog or run away to the wood, then he get licking, too. Can't be no trouble between white folks and nigger in slavery time, for they do as they choose with you. But Marster good to slave, if they done they's task and don't be up to no meanness. Missus don't have nothing to do with nigger.

In slavery, nigger go to white folks' church. Slave don't know nothing about baptizing. When nigger dead, you can't knock off work for bury 'um. You have to wait till nighttime to put 'um in the grave. You bury 'um by the light of torch. Old Man Tony Ford been the man what attend to funerals. They wasn't no nigger preacher on the plantation, but they been people to hold prayers.

I never see nigger in chain, but I see them in stock. I see plenty nigger sell on banjo [makeshift; sawhorse] table. They put you up on platform and they buy you. I see my uncle sell; he brung one hundred dollar. Woman don't sell without her chillun.

Mr. Johnnie Fripp been my young marster. When he chillun get marry, Old Marster divide the nigger. He give Marster Johnnie thirty slave, and I been one of them. Marster buy plantation on the Main [mainland]. He build big house. He have four boy and two gal. He have five hundred acre. He ain't have no overseer, just driver. We don't know no poor white trash on the Main, neither on St. Helena Island.

I work in field on Marster Johnnie Fripp plantation. Sometime we sing when us work. One song we sing been go like this:

> Go way, Old Man
> Go way, Old Man;

> Where you been all day?
> If you treat me good,
> I'll stay till the Judgment Day.
> But if you treat me bad,
> I'll sure to run away.

When war come, Missus take me and two more niggers, put we and chillun in two wagon, and go to Barnwell. My mother been one of the nigger. We stay in Barnwell all during the war. My father, he been with the Rebel, been with Mr. Marion Chaplin. When Freedom come, Missus didn't say nothing; she just cry. But she give we a wagon and we press [stole] a horse and us come back to St. Helena Island. It take three day to get home.

When we get home, we find the rest of the nigger here been have Freedom four year before we.

I work for a nigger name Peter White. My father come back and buy twenty acre of land, and we all live together. I gone to school one or two year, but I ain't learn much. Four year after war, I buy fifteen acre of land. That was this here same place where I lives now. After while I goes to work in rock [phosphate mines]. I hears about Ku Klux. They been bad people. They will kill you.

Been marry to four wife. This here last one, he been born in slavery too, but he don't remembers much about 'um. He been little gal so high, just big enough for open gate for white folks.

FANNIE GRIFFIN

Age 94, when interviewed by
Everett R. Pierce,
2125 Calhoun Street, Columbia S.C.

My marster, Marster Joe Beard, was a good man, but he wasn't one of the richest men. He only had six slaves, three men and three women. But he had a big plantation and would borrow slaves from his brother-in-law, on the adjoining plantation, to help with the crops.

I was the youngest slave, so Missy Grace, that's Marster Joe's wife, keep me in the house most of the time, to cook and keep the house cleaned up. I milked the cow and worked in the garden, too.

My marster was good to all he slaves, but Missy Grace was mean to us. She whip us a heap of times when we ain't done nothing bad to be whipped for. When she go to whip me, she tie my wrists together with a rope and put that rope through a big staple in the ceiling and draw me up off the floor and give me a hundred lashes. I think about my old mammy heap of times now and how I's seen her whipped, with the blood dripping off of her.

All that us slaves know how to do was to work hard. We never learn to read and write. Nor we never had no church to go to, only sometimes the white folks let us go to their church, but we never join in the singing. We just set and listen to them preach and pray.

The graveyard was right by the church and heap of the colored people was scared to go by it at night. They say they see ghosts and hants and spirits, but I ain't never see none, don't believe there is none. I more scared of live people than I is dead ones; dead people ain't going to harm you.

Our marster and missus was good to us when we was sick. They send for the doctor right off and the doctor do all he could for us, but he ain't had no kind of medicine to give us 'cepting spirits of turpentine, castor oil, and a little blue mass. They ain't had all kinds of pills and stuff then, like they has now. But I believe we ain't been sick as much then as we do now. I never heard of no consumption them days; us had pneumonia sometimes, though.

We never was allowed to have no parties nor dances, only from Christmas Day to New Year's Eve. We had plenty good things to eat on Christmas Day and Santa Claus was good to us, too. We'd have all kinds of frolics from Christmas to New Year's, but never was allowed to have no fun after that time.

I remembers one time I slip off from the missus and go to a dance, and when I come back, the dog in the yard didn't seem to know me and he bark and wake the missus up, and she whip me something awful. I sure didn't go to no more dances without asking her.

The patrollers would catch you, too, if you went out after dark. We most times stay at home at night and spin cloth to make our clothes. We make all our clothes, and our shoes was handmade, too. We didn't have fancy clothes like the people has now. I likes it better being a slave. We got along better then, than we do now. We didn't have to pay for everything we had.

The worst time we ever had was when the Yankee men come through. We heard they was coming, and the missus tell us to put on a big pot of peas to cook. So we put some white peas in a big pot and put a whole ham in it, so that we'd have plenty for the Yankees to eat. Then, when they come, they kicked the pot over and the peas went one way and the ham another.

The Yankees destroyed most everything we had. They come in the house and told the missus to give them her money and jewels. She started crying and told them she ain't got no money or jewels, 'cepting the ring she had on her finger. They got awfully mad and started destroying everything. They took the cows and horses, burned the gin, the barn, and all the houses 'cept the one Marster and Missus was living in.

They didn't leave us a thing 'cept some big hominy and two banks of sweet potatoes. We chipped up some sweet potatoes and dried them in the sun, then we parched them and ground them up and that's all we had to use for coffee. It taste pretty good, too. For a good while, we just live on hominy and coffee.

We ain't had no celebration after we was freed. We ain't know we was free till a good while after. We ain't know it till General Wheeler come through and tell us. After that, the marster and missus let all the slaves go 'cepting me; they kept me to work in the house and the garden.

SILVIA CHISOLM

Age 88, when interviewed by
Phoebe Faucette, in Estill, S.C., RFD.

I been eight year old when they took me. Took me
from me mother and father here on the Pipe Creek
place down to Black Swamp. Went down forty-two
mile to the overseer. Mr. Beestinger was his name.
And his wife, Miss Carrie. I was minding the overseer's chillun. Old man Joe Bostick was me marster.
And I knows the missus and the marster used to work
us. Had the overseer to drive us. Mr. Bostick was a
good old man. He been deaf. His chillun tend to his
business—his sons. He was a preacher. His father was
old man Ben Bostick.

I never see my mother or my father anymore. Not
till after Freedom. And when I come back then I been
married. But when I move back here, I stay right on
this Pipe Creek place from then on. I been right here
all the time.

The Pipe Creek Church was Old Missus Bostick's
mammy's church. When the big church burn down
by the Yankees, they give the place to the colored
folks. Stephen Drayton was the first pastor the colored
folks had. They named the church Canaan Baptist
Church. Start from a bush arbor. The white folks'

church was painted white, inside and out. It was ceiled inside.

This church didn't have no gallery for the colored folks. Didn't make no graveyard at Pipe Creek. Bury at Black Swamp. And at Lawtonville. The people leave that church and go to Lawtonville to worship. They been worshipping at Lawtonville ever since before I could wake up to know. The Pipe Creek Church just stood there, with no service in it, till the Yankee burn it. The church at Lawtonville been a fine church. Didn't burn it. Use it for a hospital during the war.

I been fifteen year old when the Yankee come— fifteen the sixth of June. I saw 'em burn down me marster's home, and everything. I remembers that. Work us till the Yankees come. When Yankee come, they had to run. That how the building burn. After they didn't find no one in it, they burn. The Marshall house had a poor white women in it. That why it didn't burn. My marster's Pineland place at Garnett was burn, too. They never did build this one back. After they come back, they build their house at the Pineland place.

After I work for Mr. Beestinger, I wait on Mr. Blunt. You know Mr. Blunt, ain't you? His place out there now.

I's eighty-eight year old now and can't remember so much. And I's blind. Blind in both eye.

PRINCE SMITH

Age 100+, when interviewed by
Augustus Ladson, on Wardmalaw Island, S.C.

I was born and raised on this island and was only from
here when the Civil War had begun. When Fort
Sumter was fired on, Marster carried seventy of us to
Greenville, South Carolina, on account of its moun-
tainous sections, which was believed would have pre-
vented the Yankee invasion in regard to their hideout.
We stayed in Greenville nearly four years. During that
time, Marster planted his farm and we work as if we
was right here.

The Yankees had gunboats, but they didn't help them
at all. They couldn't make any attack that this place is
so unsuited for water battles. But forest battles was
fight on Beaufort Island and Port Royal. We in Greenville didn't know anything about what was going on, except what was brought to us colored people by those who
was sent to the town. Marster didn't tell us anything.

For almost four years we stayed in Greenville, when
suddenly one Tuesday morning bright and early,
Sheridan came into Greenville on horsebacks and
order everybody to surrender. Colonels and generals
come in the city without the firing of a gun. We stayed
there till harvesting time by the orders of Marster

Deland Bailey, who saw to it that we was given money as a share for our work.

Marster's custom at the end of the week was to give a dry peck of corn, which you had to grind on Saturday evening when his work was done. Only on Christmas, he killed and give a piece of meat. The driver did the distribution of the ration. All young men was given four quarts of corn a week, while the grown men was given six quarts. All of us could plant as much land as we would for our own use. We could raise fowls. My marster was a gentleman; he treat all his slaves good. My father and me was his favorite.

Some of the slaves had to work on Sunday to finish their week's work. If they didn't, the driver, who was a Negro, would give a lashing varying from fifteen to twenty-five chops. Only high-class marsters had Negro drivers; the crackers had white overseers.

Like other slaves had to hide from their marsters to have meeting, we could have ours any night we want to, even without his consent. When Marster went to town, any of his slaves could ask him to buy things for them in Charleston. When Jews and peddlers come with clothes and gunger [trinkets] to sell, we as chillun would go to him and ask for money to buy what we want.

He had about four hundred acres of land, which he divided in two half by a fence. One year he would plant one and let the cattles pasture on the other. We could also raise hogs along with his, but had to change pasture when he did. The people on his plantation didn't have any need to steal from him, for he didn't allow us to want for anything.

There was three kinds of day's work on the plantation. One is the whole task, meaning a whole hand, or a person in his prime. He was given two task for his day's work. A task carried from twenty-four to twenty-five rows, which was thirty-five feet long and twenty-five feet wide. The three-fourth hand was given one whole task, which consists of twelve rows. All the young chillun was included in this group. Us half-hand was the old slaves who did a half task for their day's work.

When it was time to pick cotton, the three-fourth hand had to pick thirty pound and the half-hand twenty for their day's work. Those who attended to the gin only include the three-fourth hand.

Marster had three kinds of punishment for those who disobeyed him. One was the sweat box. That was made the height of the person and no larger. Just large enough so the person didn't have to be squeezed in. The box is nailed, and in summer is put in the hot sun; in winter it is put in the coldest, dampest place. The next is the stock. Wood is nailed on or with the person lying on his back with hands and feet tied with a heavy weight on chest. The third is the Bilbao [or bilbo: foot shackles]. You are place on a high scaffold for so many hours, and you don't try to keep a level head, you'll fall and you will surely hurt yourself, if your neck isn't broken. Most of the time they were put there so they could break their necks.

GEORGE BRIGGS

Age 88, when interviewed by
Caldwell Sims, at RFD 2, Union, S.C.;
June 1937.

Give my name right flat, it's George Briggs. Give
it round, it like this, George McDuffie Briggs.
My papa's name was Ike Wilburn, and my mother's
name was Margaret Briggs. Pa belonged to Marster
Lige Wilburn. Mama belonged to Jesse (Black Jesse)
Briggs. They both born and raised in Union
County.

I was born on Gist Briggs's plantation in Union
County, in the lower section of Cross Keys. My marster was called "Black Jesse," but the reason for that
was to keep him from getting mixed up with the other
Jesse. He was the blacksmith for all the Cross Keys
section, and for that very thing he got the name by
everybody. "Black Jesse." I always belonged to that
man and he was the kindest man what the countryside
had knowledge of.

Marster and Missus was good to us all. Missus'
name was Nancy. She die early and her grave is in
Cross Keys at the Briggs graveyard. Be still! Let me get
my mind together so that I don't get mixed up and can
get you the Briggses together. Here 'tis: Cheney and
Lucindy. Lucindy married a Floyd from Spartanburg,

and the Floyds lived at the Burnt Factory. Cheney Briggs had a son, Henry Briggs.

Not so fast, for I'm going to start way back, that time when us was little darky boys way back in slavery. When us was real little, we played horse. Before Cheney Briggs went to Arkansas, he was our play horse. His brother Henry was the wagoner and I was the mule. Henry was little and he rid our backs sometimes. Henry rid Old Man Sam, sometimes, and Old Man Sam just holler and haw-haw at us chilluns. This was in such early childhood that is not so I can exactly map out the exact age us was then. Anyway, from this we rid the gentle horses and mules and learnt how to feed them. We started to work with the marster's mules and horses.

In that day we lived in a log cabin or house. Sometimes us never had nothing to do. Our house had only one room, but some of the houses had two rooms. Ours had a window, a door, and a common fireplace. Now they makes a fireplace to scare the wood away. In old days, they made fireplaces to take care of the chilluns in the cold weather. It warm the whole house, 'cause it was so big and there was plenty wood. Wood wasn't no problem then, and it ain't no problem yet out in the lower Keys.

When I was a little shaver and come to myself, I was sleeping in a corded bed. I just studying for a minute, can't exactly identify my grandpa, but I can identify my grandma. We all raised on the same place together. I was raised strict.

When I got big and couldn't play 'round at chillun's doings, I started to plaiting corn shucks and things for making horse and mule collars, and scouring brooms and shoulder-mats. I cut hickory poles and make handles out of them for the brooms. Marster had hides tanned and us make buggy whips, wagon whips, shoestrings, saddle strings, and such as that out of our home-tanned leather. All the galluses that was wore in them days was made by the darkies.

White oak and hickory was split to cure, and we made fish baskets, feed baskets, wood baskets, sewing baskets, and all kinds of baskets for the missus. All the chair bottoms of straight chairs was made from white oak splits, and the straight chairs was made in the shop.

You make a scouring brush like this: by splitting a width of narrow splits (keep on till you lay a entire layer of splits), turn this way, then that way, and then bind together and that hold them like you want them to stay. Last, you work in a pole as long as you want it for the handle, bind it tight, and tie with the purtiest knots.

There was no church on our plantation when I was a boy. All the Baptists went to Padgett's Creek, and all the Methodist went to Quaker Church and Belmont. Padgett's Creek had a section in the back of the church for the slaves to sit. Quaker Church and Belmont both had slaves' galleries. There is a big book at Padgett's with three pages of slaves' names that was members.

Mr. Claude Sparks read it to me last year. All the darky members dead but one. That's me.

I sure can histronize the Confederates. I come along with the Secession flag and the musterings. I careful to live at home and please the marster. In the war, I's more than careful and I stick close to him and please him, and he more than good. Us did not get mobbed up like lots of them did.

Sure, I can remember when they had the mustering grounds at the Keys. There they mustered and then they turnt in and practiced drilling them soldiers till they learnt how to march and to shoot the Yankees. When these poor white men went to the war, they left their little chillun and their wives in the hands of the darkies that was kind and the rich wives of our marsters to care for. Us took the best care of them poor white that us could under the circumstances that prevailed.

I'll say it slow so that you can catch it. I start in time of the Confederate War. With dirt dug up out of the smokehouse, water was run through it so us could get salt for bread. Hickory wood ashes was used for soda. If we didn't have no hickory wood, we burnt red corn cobs; and the ashes from them we used for cooking soda.

Molasses was made from watermelons in time of the war. They was also made from May apples or May pops, as some call them, and sometimes they was made from persimmons and from wheat bran. Simmons and wheat bran are mashed up together and baked in water, let set twenty and four hours, and cook down to molasses.

In Confederate days, Irish potato tops was cooked for vegetables. Blackberry leaves was occasionally used for greens or for seasoning lambs' quarters.

They signed me to go to the Sixteenth Regiment, but I never reached the North. When us got to Charleston, us turnt around and the bosses fetched us right back to Union through Columbia. Us heard that Sherman was coming, fetching fire along behind him.

We was sent to Sullivan's Island, but before we reached it, the Yankees done got it and we won't allowed to cross in '64. But just the same, we was in service till they give Captain Franklin Bailey permission to fetch us home. There we had to git permission for everything, just as us niggers had to get permission to leave our marster's place at home in Union County. Captain Bailey come on back to Cross Keys with us under his protection, and we was under it for the longest time after we done got home.

All my life I is stayed in the fur end of Union County where it borders Laurens, with the Enoree dividing the two counties. It is right there that I is plowed and hoed and raised my crops for the past seventy-five years. I get money for plaiting galluses and making boot strings and other little things. Always first, I desires to be well qualified with what I does.

In Union County is where I was born and raised, and it's where I is going to be buried. Ain't never left the county but once in my life, and if the Lord see fitten, I ain't going to leave it no more, 'cept to reach the Promise Land. Lord, Lord, the Promise Land, that's where I is going when I leaves Union County.

ADELINE GREY

Age 82, when interviewed by
Phoebe Faucette, in Luray, S.C.

I remember when the Yankees come through. I was right to the old boss' place. It was on the river side. Miss Jane Warner, she was the missus. My ma used to belong to Old Man Dave Warner. I remember how she used to wash and iron and cook for the white folks during slavery time. The place here now, where all the chillun raise. Mr. Rhodes got a turpentine still there now, just after you pass the house.

I remember when my ma saw the Yankees coming that morning. She grab the sweet potatoes that been in that oven and throw 'em in the barrel of feathers that stayed by the kitchen fireplace. Just a barrel to hold chicken feathers when you pick 'em. That's all we had to eat that day.

They went into the company room where the old missus was staying and start tearing up the bed. Then, the captain come and the old missus say to him, "Please don't let them tear up my bed," and the captain went in there and tell them, "Come out!"

The old missus wasn't scared. But young Miss May was sure scared. She was courting at the time. She went off and shut herself up in a room. The old missus ask the captain, "Please go in and talk to the missus, she so scared." So he went in and soon he bring her out.

We chillun wasn't scared. But my brother run under the house. The soldiers went under there a-poking the bayonets into the ground to try to find where the silver buried, and they ran across him. "What you doing under here?" they say.

"I's just running the chickens out, sir," he say.

"Well, you can go on out," they say. "We ain't going to hurt you."

They choked my ma. They went to her and they say, "Where is all the white people's gold and silver?" My ma say she don't know.

"You does know," they say, and choke her till she couldn't talk.

I remember she had a red striped shawl. One of the Yankees take that and start to put it under his saddle for a saddle cloth. My brother go up to him and say, "Please sir, don't carry my ma's shawl. That the only one she got." So, he give it back to him.

They burn the ginhouse, the shop, the buggyhouse, the turkeyhouse, and the fowlhouse. Start to set the cornhouse afire, but my ma say, "Please sir, don't burn the cornhouse. Give it to me and my chillun." So, they put the fire out. I don't know why they didn't burn the house. Must have been 'cause the captain was along. The house there now. One of the chimney down. I don't think they ever put it up again. Colored folks are in it now.

I remember when they started to break down the smokehouse door, and Old Missus come out and say, "Please don't break the door open; I got the key." So they quit.

I remember when they shoot down the hog. I remember when they shoot the two geese in the yard. I remember when they kill the hog and cook 'em. Cook on the fire, where the little shop been. Cook 'em and eat 'em. Why didn't they cook 'em on the stove in the house? Didn't have no stoves. Just had to cook on the fireplace. Had an oven to fit in the fireplace.

Old Missus had give my ma a good moss mattress. But the Yankees had carry that off. Rip it up, throw out the moss, and put meat in it. Fill it full of meat. Them Yankees put the meat in the sack and go on off. It was late then, about dusk. I remember how the missus bring us all round the fire. It was dark then.

"Well chillun," she say, "I is sorry to tell you, but the Yankees has carry off your ma. I don't know if you'll ever see her anymore."

Then, we chillun all start crying. We still a-sitting there when my ma come back. She say she slip behind, and slip behind, and slip behind, and when she come to a little pine thicket by the side of the road, she dart into it, drop the sack of meat they had her carrying, and start out for home. When we had all make over her, we say to her then, "Well, why didn't you bring the sack of meat along with you?"

They took the top off Old Marster John carriage, put meat in it, and made him pull it same as a horse. Carry him way down to Lawtonville, had to pull it through the branch and all. Got the rockaway back, though—and the old man. I remember that well.

Had to mend up the old rockaway. And it made the old man sick. He keep on sick, sick, until he died. I remember how he'd say, "Don't you all worry." And he'd go out in the orchard. They'd say, "Don't bother him. Just let him be. He want to pray." After a while he died and they buried him. His name was John Stafford. They marster wasn't there. I guess he was off to the war.

I was a girl when Freedom was declared, and I can remember about the times. But, after Freedom, was the time when they suffered more than before. These chillun don't know how they blessed. To keep warm at night, they had to make their pallet down by the fire. When all wood burn out, put on another piece. Didn't have nothing on the bed to sleep on.

My ma cooked for the white folks for one year after Freedom. I remember they cook bread, and they ain't have nothing to eat on it. Was thankful for a cornbread hoecake baked in the fireplace.

But they had some things. Had buried some meat, and some syrup. And they had some corn. My ma had saved the cornhouse. The rice burn up in the gin-house.

I remember when the old missus used to have to make soap, out of these red oaks. Burn the wood, and catches the ashes. Put the ashes in a barrel with a trough under it, and pour the water through the ashes. If the lyewater that come out could cut a feather, it was strong.

Used to weave cloth after Freedom. Used to give a broach [a measurement of yarn] or two to weave at night. I's sometimes thread the needle for my ma, or pick the seed out the cotton, and make it into rolls to spin. Sometimes I'd work the foot pedal for my ma. Then they'd warp the thread.

If she want to dye it, she'd get indigo—you know that bush—and boil it. It was kinder blue. It would make good cloth. Sometimes, the cloth was kinder striped, one stripe of white, and one of blue. I remember how they'd warp the thread across the yarn after it was dyed, and I remember seeing my ma throw that shuttle through and weave that cloth.

I never did know my pa. He was sold off to Texas when I was young. My mother would say, "Well, chillun, you ain't never known your pa. Joe Smart carry him off to Texas when he went. I don't guess you'll ever see him."

My father was named Charles Smart. He never did come back. Joe Smart come back once, and say that our father is dead. He say our pa had three horses and he want one of them to be sent to us children here, but no arrangements had been made to get it to us. You see, he had chillun out there, too.

After Freedom, my ma plow many a day, same as a man, for us chillun. She work for Old Man Bill Mars. Then, she marry again. Part of the time they work for Mr. Benny Lawton, the one-arm man, what lost his arm in the war. These chillun don't know what hard times is. They don't know how to 'preciate our blessings.

SARAH POINDEXTER

Age 87, when interviewed by
Stiles M. Scruggs,
at 800 Lady Street, Columbia, S.C.

I was born in 1850, on the plantation of Jacob Poindexter, about ten miles beyond Lexington Courthouse.

The first time I see Columbia, it the powerfulest lot of big wood houses and muddy streets I ever see in my life. The Poindexter wagon, that carry my daddy, my mammy, and me to the big town, pretty often mire in mudholes all along the big road from the plantation to the courthouse. That trip was made about 1857, 'cause I was seven years old when I made that trip.

Since that first trip, I has lived in sight of Columbia, most all my life. My daddy, my mammy, and me lived on the plantation of Marster Poindexter until 1863. We might a-lived there longer, if things had not been so upset. I sure recall the excitement in the neighborhood, when roving crowds of niggers come along the big road, shouting and singing that all the niggers am free. Snow was on the ground, but the spirits of the niggers was sure plenty hot.

The Poindexter plantation was one big place of excitement them days. The slaves work some, all during the war; sometimes I now 'spects it was for the sake of the missus. All of us loved her, 'cause she was so kind and good to us. Missus Poindexter many times fetch me a piece of candy or something when she go to town and back. She was crying and worrying all the time about her menfolks, who was away fighting damn Yankees, she say.

It seem like the war last forever to me, 'stead of about five years. To a child, Lordy, how long the years hang on, and when we get past fifty, oh, how fast the time runs.

No, I never see Columbia burn in 1865, but we reckon that it was burning that night in February 1865, 'cause we smell it and the whole east look like some extra light is shining, and pretty soon, some folks come riding by and tell us the whole city in flames. The next time I see it, I guess there wasn't fifty houses standing. Chimneys standing round is about all there was, where most of the city was standing before.

My daddy was killed down about Aiken, shortly after 1865. Me and Mammy come to Columbia and live in a cabin in the alley back of Senate Street, where Mammy take in washing and cook for some white folks who know her. I helped her. She die in 1868, and I goes away with four other nigger gals to Durham to work in a tobacco factory. Both white and nigger women work there, but the nigger women do most of the hard work—stripping the leaves, stemming them, and placing them to dry. White women finish them for the trade.

In 1870, when I comes back to Columbia, the city am a-coming back. Big buildings up along the streets, but most of them was made of wood. Soon after that I gets work in a hotel, but Columbia at that time was not so big, and Durham was smaller still, although Durham had more brick houses. I was happier on the Poindexter plantation and had fewer things to worry about than when I was a-scratching around for myself.

Yes, I marry a dandy-looking young man, about my own age, about a year after I comes back to Columbia. His name, so he say, is Sam Allen. He make fun of some other niggers who work at one thing or another to live. One day he come to where I work and say he bound to raise ten dollars. I hands him the cash, and he gives me a good kiss right there before the folks, but I never see him again. I hear, after he gone, that he win some more money at a gambling place on Assembly Street, and reckon he decided to blow away, while blowing was good.

The folks who know me always call me Sarah Poindexter. I got it honestly, like other honest slaves who never know what their real name was, and so, I keeps it to the end of the road.

PETER CLIFTON

Age 89, when interviewed by
W. W. Dixon, in Winnsboro, S.C.

Yes, sir, us had a bold, driving, pushing marster, but not a hard-hearted one. I sorry when military come and arrest him.

It was this-a-way: Him try to carry on with free labor, about like him did in slavery.

Old Marster went to the field and cuss a nigger woman for the way she was working, chopping cotton. She turnt on him with the hoe and gashed him about the head with it. Him pull out his pistol and shot her. Dr. Babcock say the wound in the woman not serious. Chester was in military District No. 2. The whole state was under that military government. They swore out a warrant for Marster Biggers, arrest him with a squad, and take him to Charleston, where him had nigger jailors, and was kicked and cuffed about like a dog. They say the only thing he had to eat was cornmeal mush brought round to him and other nice white folks in a tub, and it was ladled out to them through the iron railing in the palms of their hands.

Missus stuck by him, went and stayed down there. Missus say one time they threatened her down there, that if she didn't get up ten thousand dollars they would send him where she would never see him again. The filthy prison and hard treatments broke him down. When he did get out and come home, him passed over the river of Jordan, where I hopes and prays his soul finds rest.

That was on the Biggers Mobley place, between Kershaw and Camden, where I was born, in 1848.

My marster's first wife, I heard him say, was Missus Gilmore. There was two chillun by her. Marster Ed, that live in a palace that last time I visit Rock Hill and go to remember myself to him. Then there was Miss Mary that marry her cousin, Dr. Jim Mobley. They had one child, Captain Fred, that took the Catawba Rifles to Cuba and whip Spain for blowing up the *Maine*.

Well, Marster Biggers had a big plantation and a big mansion four miles southeast of Chester. He buy my mammy and her chillun in front of the courthouse door in Chester, at the sale of the Clifton estate. Then, he turn around and buy my pappy there, 'cause my mammy and sister Lizzie was crying about him have to leave them. Mind you I wasn't born then. Marster Biggers was a widower then and went down and courted the Widow Gibson, who had a plantation and fifty slaves between Kershaw and Camden. There is where I was born.

Marster had one child, a boy, by my missus, Miss Sallie. They call him Black George. Him live long enough to marry a angel, Miss Kate McCrorey. They had four chillun. There got to be ninety slaves on the place before war come on. One time I go with pappy to the Chester place. Seem like more slaves there than on the Gibson place. Us was fed up to the neck all the time, though us never had a change of clothes. Us smell pretty rancid maybe, in the wintertime, but in the summer us not wear very much. Girls had a slip on and the boys happy in their shirt tails.

My pappy name Ned; my mammy name Jane. My brothers and sisters was Tom, Lizzie, Mary, and Gill. Us live in a log house with a plank floor and a wooden chimney, that was always catching afire and the wind coming through and filling the room with smoke and cinders. It was just one of many others, just like it, that made up the quarters. Us had peg beds for the old folks and just pallets on the floor for the chillun. Mattresses was made of wheat straw, but the pillows on the bed was cotton. I does remember that Mammy had a chicken feather pillow she made from the feathers she saved at the kitchen.

The rule on the place was: Wake up the slaves at daylight, begin work when they can see, and quit work when they can't see. But they was careful of the rule that say: You mustn't work a child, under twelve years old, in the field.

Kept foxhounds on both places. Old Butler was the squirrel and possum dog. Marster, there is nothing better than possum and yellow sweet taters. Right now, I wouldn't turn that down for pound cake and

Delaware grape wine, like my missus used to eat and sip while she watch my mammy and Old Aunt Tilda run the spinning wheels.

Marster Biggers believe in whipping and working his slaves long and hard; then a man was scared all the time of being sold away from his wife and chillun. They put the foots in a stock and clamp them together, then they have a crosspiece go right across the breast high as the shoulder. That crosspiece long enough to bind the hands of a slave to it at each end. They always strip them naked and some time they lay on the lashes with a whip, a switch, or a strap.

I see Marster buy many a slave. I never saw him sell but one, and he sold that one to a drover for $450, cash down on the table, and he did that at the request of the overseer and the missus. They was uneasy about him (the slave).

Us always have a dance in the Christmas. They give us Christmas Day. Every woman got a handkerchief to tie up her hair. Every girl got a ribbon, every boy a Barlow knife, and every man a shinplaster [refers to paper money of the time, usually devalued].

After Freedom, when us was told us had to have names, Pappy say he love his old marster Ben Clifton the best and him took that titlement, and I's been a Clifton ever since.

You ask me what for I seek out Christina for to marry. There was something about that gal, that day I meets her, though her hair had about a pound of cotton thread in it, that just attracted me to her like a fly will sail round and light on a molasses pitcher. I kept the Ashford Ferry road hot till I got her. I had to ask her old folks for her before she consent. Her have been a blessing to me every day since.

ISIAH JEFFERIES

Age 86, when interviewed by
Caldwell Sims, in Gaffney, S.C.; August 1937.

I is what is known as a outside child. I lived on the Jefferies plantation, below Wilkinsville in Cherokee County. My mother was Jane Jefferies. She was sold in slavery to Henry Jefferies. My father was Henry Jefferies. My mother had three outside chilluns, and we each had a different father.

Marster and Missus had six chilluns. Her name was Ellen and her house was three stories high. Their overseers always lived with them. There was a lot of slaves, and they all loved the white folks. The whole plantation was always up at sunup. But we did not work very late. I remember the patrollers, the Ku Klux, and the Yankees. Niggers dreaded all three. There was no jail for us: The patrollers kept us straight.

First thing I had to do as a child was to mind my ma's other chilluns, as I was the first outside one that she had. This I did until I was about twelve years old.

Ma teached me how to cook before I was twelve years old. We had good things to eat then; more than my chilluns has these times. All the slaves had their gardens on my marster's plantation. He made them do it, and they liked it. Niggers do not seem to take no pains with gardens now. Land ain't soft and mellow like it used to be. In cold weather, we had to bank out taters, rutabagas, beets, carrots, and pumpkins. The pumpkins and carrots was for the hogs and cows.

In warm weather we had cotton clothes, and in cold weather we had woolen clothes that our marster had made for us by the old ladies on the plantation. But we did go barefooted all winter until we was grown and married. We had all the wood we wanted for fire. We kept fire all day and all night. We sat by the fire in winter and popped corn, parched pinders [peanuts], and roasted corn ears.

My mother's husband was named Ned. Before her marriage, she was a Davis. I always lived with my mother, and Ned was as good to me as he was to his own chillun. After she married Ned, then he jest come to be our pa—that is, he let her give us his name. She and Ned had four chillun.

My ma and Ned was working one day and I was minding her chilluns as usual, when I looked up and seed the top of our house on fire. I hollered, and they come running from the field. The other hands come with them, 'cause I made such a noise hollering. Soon, the big folks got the fire out. After that, Marster Henry had me to leave the house and go to work for him.

It was spring, and I started in chopping cotton. Appears that I got on pretty well, and that the overseer

liked me from the start. From there on, I was broke
into field work of all kinds, and then I did work around
the lot, as well. It was not long before everybody started calling me Uncle Zery—why, I did not know, but
anyway, that name still sticks to me by them that
knows me well.

My grandpa never called me that, 'cause I was
named after him and he too proud of that fact to call
me any nickname. I stayed with him at his house lots
after I started working for the marster, 'cause he
showed me how to do things. I worked for him to get
my first money, and he would give me a quarter for a
whole day's work. That made me feel good, and I
thought I was a man 'cause I made a quarter.

In them days, a quarter was a lot of money. I spent
it for chewing tobacco, and that made me sick at first.
That's all men had to spend money for in them days.
Everything was give you on the plantation, and you
did not need much money. Sometimes we cooked out
in the field, and I have cooked bread in the field in a
lid.

When I got to be a big boy, my ma got religion at
the camp meeting at El-Bethel. She shouted and sung
for three days, going all over the plantation and the
neighboring ones, inviting her friends to come to see
her baptized, and shouting and praying for them.

She went around to all the people that she had done
wrong and begged their forgiveness. She sent for them
that had wronged her and told them that she was born

again and a new woman, and that she would forgive them. She wanted everybody that was not saved to go up with her.

The white folks was baptized in the pool first, and then their darkies. When the darkies' time come, they sung and shouted so loud that the patrollers come from somewhere, but Marster and Missus made them go away and let us shout and rejoice to the fullest.

Missus had all her darkies that was a-going in for baptizing to wear white calico in the pool. In the sewing room, she had had calico robes made for everybody. My ma took me with her to see her baptized, and I was so happy that I sung and shouted with her. All the niggers joined in singing. The white folks stayed and saw us baptize our folks, and they liked our singing.

My first wife is dead and my second wife is named Alice Jefferies. I got one child by my first wife, and I ain't got no outside chilluns. That works out bad, at best. None of my folks is living. All of them is done dead now. Just me, my wife, and my sister's daughter, Emma, who is grown now. Her pa and her ma took and went crazy before they died. Both of them died in the asylum. We took Emma, and she ain't just exactly right; but she ain't no bother to us.

ROBERT TOATLEY

Age 82, when interviewed by
W. W. Dixon, near White Oak, S.C.

I was born on the Elizabeth Mobley place. Us always called it Cedar Shades. There was a half-mile of cedars on both sides of the road leading to the fine house that our white folks lived in.

My marster was rich. Slaves lived in quarters, three hundred yards from the big house. A street run through the quarters, homes on each side. Beds was homemade. Mattresses made of wheat straw. Bed covers was quilts and counterpanes, all made by slave women.

Never had any money, didn't know what it was. Mammy was a housewoman, and I got just what the white chillun got to eat, only a little bit later, in the kitchen. There was fifty or sixty other little niggers on the place. Want to know how they was fed? Well, it was like this: You've seen pig troughs, side by side, in a big lot? After all the grown niggers eat and get out the way, scraps and everything eatable was put in them troughs. Sometimes buttermilk poured on the mess and sometimes potlicker. Then, the cook blowed a cow horn. Quick as lightning a passel of fifty or sixty little niggers run out the plum bushes, from under the sheds and houses, and from everywhere. Each one take his place and souse his hands in the mixture and eat just like you see pigs shoving around slop troughs.

The biggest whipping I ever heard tell of was when they had a trial of several slave men for selling liquor at the spring, during preaching, on Sunday. The trial come off at the church about a month later. They was convicted, and the order of the court was: Edmund to receive 100 lashes, Sam and Andy each 125 lashes, and Frank and Abram 75 lashes. All to be given on their bare backs and rumps, well laid on with strap. If the courts would sentence like that these days, there'd be more attention to the law.

My white folks, the Mobleys, made us work on Sunday sometime, with the fodder, and when the plowing get behind. They mighty neighborly to rich neighbors but didn't have much time for poor buckra. I tell you, poor white men have poor chance to rise, make something and be something, before the old war. Some of these same poor buckra done had a chance since then and they way up in G [government] now. They mighty nigh run the county and town of Winnsboro, plum mighty nigh it, I tell you.

My missus was a daughter of Dr. John Glover. When her oldest child, Sam, come back from college, he fetched a classmate, Jim Carlisle, with him. That boy, Jim, made his mark, got religion, and went to the top of a college in Spartanburg. Marster Sam study to be a doctor. He start to practice, and then he marry

Miss Lizzie Rice down in Barnwell. Missus give me to them, and I went with them and stayed till Freedom.

'Twas not till the year of '66 that we got reliable information and felt free to go where us pleased to go. Most of the niggers left, but Mammy stayed on and cooked for Dr. Sam and the white folks.

Bad white folks comed and got bad niggers started. Soon, things got wrong and the devil took a hand in the mess. Out of it come to the top the carpetbag, the scalawags, and then the Ku Klux. Night rider come by and drop something at your door and say, "I'll just leave you something for dinner." Then ride off in a gallop. When you open the sack, what you reckon in there? One time it was six nigger heads that was left at the door.

Was it at my house door? Oh, no! It was at the door of a nigger too active in politics. Old Congressman Wallace sent Yankee troops, three miles long, down here. Lots of white folks was put in jail.

I married Emma Greer in 1870; she been dead two years. Us lived husband and wife fifty-six years, bless God. Us raised ten chillun; all is going well. All us Presbyterians. Can read, but can't write. Our slaves was told if ever they learned to write, they'd lose the hand or arm they wrote with.

SYLVIA CANNON

Age 85, when interviewed by
Annie Ruth Davis, at Marion Street,
Florence S.C.; October 1937.

I don't know exactly how old I is 'cause the peoples used to wouldn't tell they chillun how old they was before they was grown. There been about fourteen head of we chillun, and they all gone but me. I the last one.

Yes, ma'am, I been a little small girl in slavery time. I just can remember when I was sold. Me and Becky and George. Just can remember that, but I know who bought me. First belong to the old Bill Greggs, and that where Miss Earlie Hatchel bought me from. Never did know where Becky and George went.

I see 'em sell plenty colored peoples away in them days, 'cause that the way white folks made heap of they money. Course, they ain't never tell us how much they sell 'em for. Just stand 'em up on a block about three feet high and a speculator bid 'em off just like they was horses. Them what was bid off didn't never say nothing neither. Don't know who bought my brothers, George and Earl.

I see 'em sell some slaves twice before I was sold, and I see the slaves when they be traveling like hogs to

Darlington. Some of them be women folks looking like they going to get down, they so heavy.

Yes, ma'am, the Bill Greggs had a heap of slaves 'cause they had my grandmammy and my granddaddy and they had a heap of chillun. My mammy, she belong to the Greggs, too. She been Mr. Greggs's cook, and I the one name after her. I remembers she didn't talk much to we chillun. Mostly, she did sing about all the time.

> Oh Heaven, sweet Heaven,
> When shall I see?
> If you get there before me,
> You tell my Lord I on the way.

Oh, that be a old song what my grandmammy used to sing way back there.

The white folks didn't never help none of we black people to read and write no time. They learn the yellow chillun, but if they catch we black chillun with a book, they nearly 'bout kill us. They was sure better to them yellow chillun than the black chillun that be on the plantation. Northern women come there after the war, but they didn't let 'em teach nobody nothing.

Father and Mother belong to the old Bill Greggs and that where Miss Earlie Hatchel buy me from. After that, I didn't never live with my parents anymore, but I went back to see them every two weeks. Got a note and go on a Sunday evening and come

back to Miss Hatchel on Monday. Miss Hatchel want
a nurse and that howcome she buy me.

I remembers Miss Hatchel putting the baby in my
lap and tell me don't drop him. Didn't have to do no
work much in them days, but they didn't allow me to
play none neither. When the baby sleep, I sweep the
yard, work the garden, and pick seed out the cotton to
spin. Oh, honey, there won't no such thing as cotton
mill, train, sawmill, or nothing like that in my day.
People had to sit there at night and pick the seed out
the cotton with they own hands.

We lived in the quarter about one-half mile from
the white folks' house in a one-room pole house what
was daubed with dirt. There was about twenty other
colored people house there in the quarter. The ground
been us floor and us fireplace been down on the
ground. Take sticks and make chimney, 'cause there
won't no bricks and won't no sawmills to make lumber
when I come along.

Oh, my white folks live in a pole house daubed with
dirt, too. Us just had some kind of homemade bedstead with pine straw bed what to sleep on in them
days. Sew croaker [burlap] sack together and stuff 'em
with pine straw. That how they make they mattress.

Didn't get much clothes to wear in that day and
time neither. Man never wear no breeches in the
summer. Go in his shirttail that come down to the
knees and a woman been glad enough to get one-piece
homespun frock what was made with they hand.

Make petticoat out of old dress and patch and patch till couldn't tell which place weave. Always put wash out on a Saturday night and dry it and put it back on Sunday. Then get oak leaves and make a hat what to wear to church.

I go to church with my white folks, but they never have no church like they have these days. The bush was they shelter, and when it rain, they meet 'round from one house to another. Ride to church in the ox cart, 'cause I had to carry the baby everywhere I go. White folks didn't have no horse then.

Marster and Missus taught me to say a prayer that go like this:

> The angels in Heaven love us,
> Bless Mamma and bless Papa,
> Bless our Missus,
> Bless the man that feeding us,
> For Christ sake.

We didn't never have but one pair of shoes a year, and they was these here brogans with thick soles and brass toes. Had shop there on the plantation where white man made all the shoes and plows. They would save all the cowhide and soak it in salt two or three weeks to get the hair off it. They have big trough hewed out where they clean it after they get the hair off it. After that, it was turn to the man at the shop.

Oh, yes, they have white overseers then. I hear some people say they was good people. At night the overseer would walk out to see could he catch any of us walking without a note, and to this day, I don't want to go nowhere without a paper.

It just like this: The overseer didn't have to be right behind you to see that you work in them days. They have all the fields named and the overseer just had to call on the horn and tell you what field to go work in that day. Then, he come along on a Saturday evening to see what you done.

Yes, ma'am, white folks had to whip some of they niggers in slavery time; they be so mean. Some was mean 'cause they tell stories on one another and been swear to it. My mammy tell me don't never tell nothing but the truth and I won't get no whipping.

I remembers when night come on and we go back to the quarter, we cook bread in the ashes and pick seed from the cotton. My mama sat there and sew heap of the time. Then, I see 'em when they have them hay pullings. They tote torch to gather the hay by. After they pull two or three stacks of hay, they have a big supper, dance in the road, beat sticks, and blow cane. Had to strike fire on cotton with two rocks, 'cause they didn't have no match in them days.

We fare good in that day and time. They never whip me in all my life. Tell me if I don't know how to do anything to tell them, and they show me how. I remembers Miss Hatchel caught and shook me one time, and when I tell her husband, he tell her to keep her hands off his little nigger. They all was good to me. When I start home to see my mama, they cry after me till I come back.

Folks eat all kind of things during the war. Eat honeysuckle off the low sweet bush after the flower falls off and pine nuts that they get out the burr and sour weeds. Wouldn't nobody eat them things these days. Course, they let the slaves have three acres of land to a family to plant for they garden. Work them in moonlight nights and on a Saturday evening.

I telling you my missus sure was good to me in that day and time. She been so good to me that I stay there with her twenty year after I got free. Stay there till I marry the old man Isenia Cannon. You see my old marster got killed in the war. She tell me I better stay where I can get flour bread to eat, 'cause she make her own flour and bake plenty biscuit in the oven. Then, she kill hogs and a cow every Christmas and give us all the eggnog and liquor we want that day. Dig hole in the ground and roast cow over log fire.

When I get hard up for meat and couldn't get nothing else, I catch rabbits and birds. Make a death trap with a lid, bait it with cabbage and corn, and catch them that way. Then another time, I dig deep hole in the ground and daub it with clay and fill it up with water. Rabbits hunt water in the night, fall in there, and drown. I used to set traps heap of times to keep the rabbits from eating up the people gardens.

My son born in the year of the earthquake [1886], and if he had lived, I would been blessed with plenty grandchillun these days. I remember all about the shake. They tell me one man, Mr. Turner, give away his dog two or three days before the earthquake come on. That dog get loose and come back the night of the shake.

Come back with chain tied round his neck, and Mr. Turner been scared most to death, so they tell me. He say, "Oh, Mr. Devil, don't put the chain on me, I'll go with you." That was his dog come back and he thought it was the devil come there to put the chain on him.

Didn't hear tell about no telephone nowhere in them days, and people never live no closer than three and four miles apart neither. Got Old Marster horn right in that room there now that he could talk on to people that be sixteen miles from where he was. Come in here, child, and I'll let you see it.

See, this old horn been made out of silver money. You talks in that little end and what you say runs out that big end. Man ask me didn't I want to sell it, and I tell him I ain't got no mind to get rid of it 'cause it been belong to Old Marster. Then, if I get sick, I call on it and somebody come. I sold Old Marster's sword last week for ten cents, but I ain't going do away with his old horn. It the old-time phone. Got Old Marster's maul, too, and this here Grandpa oxen bit that was made at home.

The peoples use herb medicines that they get out the woods for they cures in them days. I make a herb medicine that good for anything. Couldn't tell you how I make it 'cause that would ruin me. Town people try to buy the remedy from me, but Dr. McLeod tell me not to sell it.

Times was sure better long time ago than they be now. I know it. Colored people never had no debt to pay in slavery time. Never hear tell about no colored people been put in jail before Freedom. Had more to eat and more to wear then, and had good clothes all the time 'cause white folks furnish everything, everything. Had plenty peas, rice, hog meat, rabbit, fish, and such as that.

Had they extra crop what they had time off to work every Saturday. White folks tell them: What they made, they could have. Peoples would have found we colored people rich with the money we made on the extra crop, if the slaves hadn't never been set free. Us had big rolls of money, and then when the Yankees come and change the money, that what made us poor.

It let the white people down and let us down, too. Left us all to about starve to death. Been force to go to the fish pond and the huckleberry patch. Land went down to a dollar a acre. White people let us clear up new land and make us own money that way. We bury it in the ground and that howcome I had money. I dig mine up one day and had over fifteen hundred dollars that I been save. People back there didn't spend money like they do these days and that howcome I had that money. They would just spend money once a year in that day and time.

Rich man up there in Florence learn about I was worth over fifteen hundred dollars, and he tell me that I ought to buy a house, that I was getting old. Say he had a nice place he want to sell me. He say, "Mom Sylvia, you stay here long as you live, 'cause you ain't going be here much longer."

Yes, ma'am, I pay that man over nine hundred dollars. Been paying on it long time and got it all paid but $187 and city find out what that man had done. I thought this house been belong to me, but they tell me this here place be city property. I been trust white folks and he take my money and settle me down here on city property.

City tell me just stay on right here, but don't pay no more money out. I beg the town to let me go out to the poor farm and stay, but they say I done pay too much to move. Tell me stay on here and keep the house up the best way I can. They give me that garden and tell me what I make I can have.

I promise my God right then not to save no more money, child. If the town picks up any sick person, they bring them here and tell me do the best I can for them. City tell me do like I was raised and so I been chopping here about twenty years.

I ain't able to do no kind of work much. No more than chopping my garden. Can't hardly see nothing on a sunny day. I raise my own seed all right, 'cause sometimes I can't see and find myself is cut up things, and that make me has to plant over another time.

The peoples sure been blessed with more religion in them days than these days. Didn't never have to look up nothing then, and if you tell a story, you get a whipping. Now, the peoples tell me to tell a story. I been cleaning up a lady porch and she tell me to tell anybody what come there that she ain't home.

A lady come and ask for her, and I tell her, "She say anybody come here, tell 'em 'I ain't home.' If you don't believe she here, look in the bedroom."

Miss Willcox come out there and beat me in the back. I tell her, "Don't read the Bible and tell me to tell a story. I ain't going tell no story, 'cause my white folks learnt me not to do that."

SAVILLA BURRELL

Age 83, when interviewed by
W. W. Dixon, in Winnsboro, S.C.

My marster in slavery time was Captain Tom Still. He had big plantation down there on Jackson Creek. My missus's name was Mary Ann, though she wasn't his first wife—just a second wife, and a widow when she captivated him. You know widows is like that anyhow, 'cause they done had experience with mens and wraps them round their little finger and get them under their thumb before the mens knows what going on. Young gals have a poor chance against a young widow like Miss Mary Ann was. Her had her troubles with Marster Tom after her get him, I tell you, but maybe best not to tell that, right now anyways.

Marster Tom had four chillun by his first wife. They was John, Sam, Henrietta, and I can't remember the name of the other one, least right now. They teached me to call chillun three years old Young Marster, and say Missie. They whip you if they ever hear you say Old Marster or Old Missie. That riled them.

My pappy name Sam; my mother name Mary. My pappy did not live on the same place as Mother. He was a slave of the Hamiltons, and he got a pass sometimes to come and be with her, not often. Grandmammy name Esther, and she belonged to our marster Tom Still, too.

Us lived in a log cabin with a stick chimney. The bed was nailed to the side of the walls. Just one room.

Never seen any money. Us half-naked all the time. Grown boys went around barefooted and in their shirttail all the summer. There was plenty to eat such as it was, but in the summertime, before us get there to eat, the flies would be all over the food and some was swimming in the gravy and milk pots. Marster laughed about that and say it made us fat.

Marster was a rich man. He had a big gin house and sheep, goats, cows, mules, horses, turkeys, geese, and a stallion named Stocking-Foot. Us little niggers was scared to death of that stallion. Mothers used to say to chillun to quiet them, "Better hush, Stocking-Foot will get you and tramp you down." Any child would get quiet at that.

Old Marster was the daddy of some mulatto chillun. The relations with the mothers of those chillun is what give so much grief to Missus. The neighbors would talk about it, and he would sell all them chillun away from they mothers to a trader. My missus would cry about that. They sell one of Mother's chillun once, and when she take on and cry about it, Marster say, "Stop that sniffing there if you don't want to get a whipping." She grieve and cry at night about it.

Our doctor was old Marster's son-in-law, Dr. Martin. I seen him cup a man once. He was a good doctor. He give slaves castor oil, bleed them sometimes, and make them take pills.

Us looked for the Yankees on that place like us look now for the Savior and the host of angels at the Second Coming. They come one day in February. They took everything carryable off the plantation and burnt the big house, stables, barns, gin house. They left the slave houses.

After the war, I marry Osborne Burrell and live on the Tom Jordan place. I's the mother of twelve chillun. Just three living now. I lives with the Mills family three miles above town. My son Willie got killed at the DuPont Powder Plant at Hopewell, Virginia, during the World War.

Young Marster Sam Still got killed in the Civil War. Old Marster live on. I went to see him in his last days, and I sat by him and kept the flies off while there. I see the lines of sorrow had plowed on that old face, and I remembered he'd been a captain on horseback in that war. It come into my remembrance the song of Moses: "The Lord had triumphed glorily and the horse and his rider have been throwed into the sea."

A Note on the Type

The text of this book was set in Electra, a typestyle designed by William Addison Dwiggins, a pre-eminent type and book designer. Its sharp, flat serifs give it brilliant calligraphic features.

Composed by The Composing Room of
Michigan, Grand Rapids, Michigan

Printed and bound by Edwards Brothers
Lillington, North Carolina

Book design by
Debra L. Hampton